PRAISE FOR SUEBIQUITOUS

D1541319

"Sue is the funniest woman I know and she has wrapped up all that hilarity in SUEbiquitous. You need this book like you need chocolate and long talks with your best friend. If you don't laugh until you cry then you may need to see a doctor."

—ALLI WORTHINGTON,
AUTHOR OF *BREAKING BUSY:
HOW TO FIND PEACE AND
PURPOSE IN A WORLD OF CRAZY*

"Full of wit, truth and a few miracles, Suebiquitous, had me at the first line. Duffield's story is engaging and fun. Sue's the kind of woman we all want as our girlfriend. Personal stories woven through with spiritual truth. A perfect read."

—RACHEL HAUCK,
NEW YORK TIMES BESTSELLING AUTHOR
OF *THE WEDDING DRESS*

"I love Sue Duffield! She is a friend-raiser for Jesus! This book is full of stories, musings and gentle exhortations that highlight her 'Sue-niqueness' in this world. You will chuckle, smile, and shake your head while reading. You'll turn the last page wishing for more. Sue gives us hope that our uniqueness too can be used for God's glory!"

—CANDY DAVISON,
WOMEN'S MINISTRY COORDINATOR
OF SANDY COVE MINISTRIES, MD

"For nearly 40 years Christian speaker, singer, and all-around joy bringer Sue Duffield has touched hearts (and funny bones) of women worldwide. In *SUEbiquitious*, with generosity and transparency, Duffield takes her bravery and brilliance from the stage to the page. Prepare to laugh, to cry, and to be SUEpernaturally inspired as you travel these pages alongside your new best friend. Be it a plane ride, a restaurant, an everyday encounter, or an auditorium filled with women, Duffield's signature cocktail of humor, wisdom, and compassion never fails to reach and teach God's beloved."

—TONI BIRDSONG,
COMMUNICATION STRATEGIST,
AND AUTHOR OF *STICKY JESUS*

"In this uniquely zany road trip, Sue Duffield prays, 'God, help me to know that the biggest and best challenge will be the fight to be real.' Guess what? God answers that prayer for Sue—as He does for all who ask—with a lifetime of adventures and laughter and fun stories."

—JO KADLECEK,
AUTHOR OF *WOMAN OVERBOARD:
HOW PASSION SAVED MY LIFE*

"Sue has been a dear friend for many years. Always quick with a wisecrack, smile or prayer; she is one devoted woman to Jesus. I vividly remember her on a small local radio station in the beginning. That voice, that wit and charm; always warm and sunny. Then I heard her sing and I was hooked! WOW! What a voice, combined with a spirituality that I just knew was a special gift. Her story here is wonderful. What's missing is her visual silliness but not her "genuineness." After you experience SUEbiquitous's heart, mind, and funny bone, then listen to her sing. You will treasure both."

—FRED DAWSON,
WEALTH MANAGER OF BASSETT,
DAWSON & FOY, INC.

"Sue Duffield is one of the funniest, craziest people I have ever met. She is the real deal. Her laughter and smile are infectious, but her love for Jesus is contagious. She has the ability to make you laugh and yet she has the gift of getting down to the real issues when it comes to our walk with Jesus. Any journey with Sue will be worth the trip."

—BILL WELTE,
PRESIDENT/CEO OF AMERICA'S
KESWICK, WHITING NJ

"By the time you finish this book, you will have laughed and cried your way to a healthy dose of God's amazing grace. Women struggle with the comparison trap and being status quo but Sue shows us we need to be comfortable in our own skin. We are God's creation and He loves us simply for that reason. Grab this book, sit back and be ready for a dose of the daily, droll and divine - all in one - as she "bares" all."

—REV. LINDA MORRISON,
NY WOMEN OF PURPOSE DIRECTOR,
NY MINISTRY NETWORK

"Sue Duffield is truly one of a kind. In our years of working with hundreds of people, she stands alone in her ability to bring out the "funny" in life. Her humor is so completely contagious that, after spending time with her, we find that there seems to be a "Sue aftereffect" which causes us to look at life through a different lens - the lens of laughter. Sue has a way of cutting through the rhetoric down to the heart of the matter. While you're laughing with her (or really at her) she is expertly probing the real issues of life and exposing them to God's healing with the skillfulness of a surgeon."

—PASTOR ALAN & DONNA BOSMENY

SUEbiquitous

—a Humorous Travelog of an Unfiltered Saint

SUE DUFFIELD

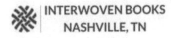

INTERWOVEN BOOKS
NASHVILLE, TN

Ordering Information:
Special discounts are available on quantity purchases by churches, corporations, associations, and others. For details, contact the publisher at the address above or visit www.interwovenbooks.com.

Cover design: Micah Kandros Design
Interior design: Brian Mast

Manufactured in the United States of America
10 9 8 7 6 5 4 3 2 1
Library of Congress Cataloging-in-Publication data
Duffield, Sue. Suebiquitous: A Humorous Travelog of an Unfiltered Saint / Sue Duffield. pages cm. Duffield, Sue 2. Christian Biography 3. Humor 4. Christian Life-Miscellanea. I. Title
Library of Congress Control Number: 2016938939
ISBN: 978-0-9975114-0-6

DEDICATION

For my parents, Al and Naomi Beatty,
who left this earth, but never left me.

CONTENTS

FOREWORD BY TAMI HEIM

President and CEO of Christian Leadership Alliance

Hugh Sidney was a journalist for *Life* and *Time* Magazines in years close to when Sue and I were born. He once said,

> "Above all else: go out with a sense of humor. It is needed armor. Joy in one's heart and some laughter on one's lips is a sign that the person down deep has a pretty good grasp of life."

And so it is true of my beloved friend, Sue Duffield. Gifted with talents galore, she uses them to paint a perspective about living that jiggles your spirit and tickles your heart. With humor in a perfect pitch, she amplifies the God-connections between this life and the one that's to come.

Yes, you can say, she has a *pretty good grasp of life*.

I met *SUEweet* Sue in 2009. With the stroke of her keypad and the release of a single tweet, she tattooed a smile on my heart. God knew it was the perfect time to connect His Jersey girl with this

Hoosier hayseed and used a Michigan cider mill to close the deal.

Since that first tweet we've shared a lot of life. We've laughed, cried laughing, and almost died laughing. *Can you say road trip?* We've prayed through tough stuff, and wept over many a holy moment. And we held hands, awestruck as the gaze of God beheld us through the eyes of orphans in Haiti.

I love that the significance of *every* moment is never lost on Sue. You will find this truth about her embedded in the words of *every* page. She notices what some of us cannot and makes us better because of it. Sue has taught me to value and see things simply; like packing extra extension cords for travel in a third-world country, the knowledge that Georgia actually touches the Atlantic Ocean, and that there is beauty in every life if you will risk opening your heart to receive it.

There could not be a more perfect title for this book than *SUEbiquitious* because it is SO Sue. Once you meet her, you'll find her everywhere, anywhere, and completely immersed in whatever she is doing. Jim Elliot, an evangelical Christian who was one of five missionaries killed while attempting to evangelize the Huaorani people of Ecuador, exhorted others by saying, "Wherever you are, be all there! Live to the hilt every situation you believe to be the will of God." Sue is my constant reminder of what happens when someone lives life this way.

I stand amazed by what God will do when we take the time to enter the portals He's created in this time and place through technology. He gives us abundant opportunities to peek deep into the souls of others if we just slow down long enough to pay attention to them. I am excited for you. Now you have a chance to peak into the heart and soul of my *SUEsational* friend.

I pray that as you read this book, you will laugh hard and often, catch joy, learn much, and long earnestly for the Spirit of God to move in your life.

Now, get ready.

SUEbiquitous has arrived with a special delivery, wrapped in loving laughter, and sealed with a special mark that's just for you.

> *He will yet fill your mouth with laughter*
> *and your lips with a shout of joy.*
> *~ Job 8:21, HCSB*

CHAPTER ONE

"tSUEnami"

I'm boarding Korean Airlines Flight #7890 in Atlanta, flying through Seoul en route to Malaysia. I plan the fourteen hours out to read, write, eat, sleep, watch a few movies, and inhale the aroma of jasmine surrounding me. It's quite intoxicating and smell-licous, like a combination of spices from the food ready to be served, maybe, and/or a combination of cleaning cloths and gardenia-scented soaps to be handed out to passengers for cleanup? I'm not sure, but either way the aroma is distinctly different, distinctly Korean, and so not like the ATL airport whiff or jet-way fuel reek I've just stepped away from.

I have eight hundred forty minutes to write in my journal. I have plans to write a book some day, and writing in my journal is the way I chip away toward the goal to somehow capture the nutty tsunami that is my experience. This tidal wave of a life represents multiple crazy quakes and humorous landslides. The first victim of the tsunami that is Sue Duffield was my dear mother.

I pushed my way out of my mother like a cataclysmic eruption. She said I was making my rumbling presence known in her belly as the winds of hurricane Connie ripped through our small Jersey county. That hot and sticky August day in 1955, plus the smell of new paint in my parents' kitchen, sent my mother into early labor. The nurses insisted they should name me Connie, but my dad had other plans. I know he wished I had been a Connor or Conrad, but he appeared to be content with his little black-eyed Susan.

The story goes that when Grand-pop Link heard the news, he blurted out, "Praise the Lord, we have a Susan Lee!"

Silly man. What in the world? Silent Pop Link actually expressed himself? That very unusual verbal eruption spewed from a happy little quiet man who was known to rarely talk, let alone shout.

Sue Lee. Sounds kind of Asian, doesn't it? Do I dare tell you the family joke that surfaces here? Sure, why not?

My dad's early rebellious days before his Navy stint in Korea may surprise you, especially if you knew him only as an adult. His adolescent life was less than exemplary—a jokester, a prankster, an underage drunk and a climbing graffiti-champ of the Carneys Point water tower. But Albert "Bunky" Beatty later became a rock of faith to his family, his arsenal of friends, and his enormous extended community. No one climbed higher than my dad, morally. Still, we teased him by saying he may have played around too much with those cute Korean girls during the war. Maybe I have a brother or sister named Kwang Beatty-sun. It's pretty farfetched, but it always got a laugh. Never funny, though, to my mother.

This trip down memory lane is taking up space in my head as I make my way up the aisle of the plane. I'll soon be sailing through the atmosphere on a self-made missions trip to visit my Jersey friends Carrie and Mindy and the rescued girls of a safe house they run in Kuala Lumpur. Carrie's mom, Barb, was one of my mom's best friends, so we go way back. This trip feels very full-circle, as Mom is on my mind. The first thing on my agenda is engaging with the cast of characters on this floating airship.

As I find my seat, an elegant Korean Air flight attendant says, "Hello. I'm Yeun. You name?"

Her beauty stuns me, completely. I can't help but stare and stutter.

"Sue Lee," I say, hoping to raise her perfect eyebrows. This woman is breathtaking—tall, slender, a sort of sultry hybrid of Audrey Hepburn and Jin-Soo Kwon (you know, Jin and Sun, the doomed couple on LOST?). I ask to snap a quick photo.

She poses like a picture from *Life Magazine*, holding her hand like a fan to her face. Batting her eyes with a half smirk she says, "Hmm. You no look much like a Sue Lee, but I go with it."

I pause to think of something clever to say. "Does it help that I love curry and all things Southeast Asian? I think I may have been Korean in my former life." Oh, brother. That was dumb. I know better than to say something stupid like that. Not only is my cultural filter broken, but I find out later that I puff up like a blowfish when I come anywhere near curry. And Malaysian curry, at that!

Yeun looks down at me, and frowns. "Well, it does help, but you need much more tiny body, more darker hair and pale skin. You smell like donut. You too much Ahhnn Mah-ree."

I don't know what an Ahhnn Mah-ree is, until my seatmate says, "She trying to say *Anne Murray*."

I laugh to myself. I'm Anne Murray! Yeah, I'm a snowbird, all right. (*Snowbird* was Anne's best top-40 hit, in case you were born after a certain date in the last century). I totally deserve this. I crack up, throw my head back, and slap my knee. And I am suddenly aware how my mannerism mirrors my mother. Definitely something my mother would do: slap her knee, roll her eyes, and catapult her head back and forth in agreement with you or when she thought you caught onto something.

Eastern culture adores American music, and it matters not the genre or age; current or retro. Pop artists like Richard Carpenter, Christopher Cross, Donna Summer, and countless other musical icons continue to make serious money through music sales on foreign soil. And truth is, the Eastern Hemisphere appreciates all styles of American music. We're too fickle in the States, with the current glitzy strand and direction of pop music. If it's old or dated, it's less desired.

So Anne Murray *is* a big deal in Korea and quite the fun thing to say to a white, plump American. Yeun not only cracks me up; she's sharp. Her smarts are a match for my sass. We're already way past politically correct. The age difference, the donut smell remark, and my stereotype of Asians get us off on the right (and so wrong) foot. What we have here is the perfect climate for some rip-roaring fun on a long overseas flight.

"And you haven't even heard me sing yet!" I say, all braggadocios as I unload pens, journals, a Bible, and a Ziploc bag of wasabi peas from my backpack onto my lap.

"Ohhh!" Yeun's voice rises and falls. "You singer, too? I bet you sing like Ahhnn Mah-ree too, no?"

"No. I much better," I say.

"You make me fun, Sue Lee?" She laughs.

"Yes, I hope to *make you fun*, Yen, Yern, Yeun—whatever your name is."

I might be in trouble now. She gives me a playful smack on the back of my head, laughing and walking away.

I close my eyes; lay my head back, and visualize myself on stage with Anne Murray. I'm the backup singer; Anne's the star and I see Yeun running around the stage with a clipboard and a headset microphone, shouting, "This all wrong! This all wrong! Sue Lee should be star! She make better music than Ahhnn Mah-ree! She smells like donut, but no give her curry!"

Trying to get comfy in Economy is like wedging my body into a Coleman cooler. I should have spent the extra $2000 for Business Class. Yeun walks by. I say out loud as she walks right past me, "Hey! Yeun! Are flight attendants nicer in Business?"

"Sue Lee, you be careful. I put you out on wing. Lots of nice airy kind of comfy out there."

This whirlwind of good-humored jabbing between Yeun and me is just gearing up. I get some of my best material simply by engaging with people. Yeun's and my exchange is fast, furious, and fun—a typical outcome of my tSUEnamic kind of personality.

A real tsunami is no laughing matter. It will wipe out everything in its path. The devastation of the rising ocean brings on an even more critical threat: *If you don't drown in the water, you will surely die from the debris—boats, cars, timber and other things that can take you out.* It took me years to figure this out. My extroverted tendencies will wipe out a room of introverts. The debris I have been known to leave behind is lost love and disillusioned friendships. I have good intentions but am still learning how to channel this tSUEnami.

I don't know when I first realized this all-about-me consuming behavior, but it was pretty obvious early on. Like a whirling dervish, my loud obnoxious presence could be both violently amazing and spectacularly awful at the same time. My kindergarten teacher knew she must somehow contain me. I sang the loudest, talked the loudest and could barely keep my hands to myself. Hugging everything that moved was a genetic thing. Too touchy-feely. Which could be both endearing and a little scary at the same time. I was a strong little girl who trusted everyone. I just knew the whole world loved me; it was a foregone conclusion. I made friends fast because of my rambunctious and uninhibited laugh. I was a tangy mix of tomboy and prissy girl who wanted to be the life of the romper room party.

My third grade teacher, Mrs. Davis, saw something in me, I'm told. She was the teacher with the braided gray-haired bird's nest on top of her head. Seems right she would be the one to give me hope. I liked bird's nests. We weren't too sure what that "saw something in me" meant. Maybe she saw in me the potential for my, er, *large* personality to morph into a commanding presence one day.

I was short in stature, but because I sang so loud, my music teacher relegated me to the back row, standing on a stool. Oh, and my music teacher was the *other* Davis. [It was very confusing for an eight-year-old to have two Davis teachers, but believe me, they were nothing alike. Miss *Hazel Ann* Davis loved Jesus. Bird's Nest Mrs. *Ivie Jane* Davis loved JFK.] My singing was known to wipe out a few kid singers in front of me. And if I didn't knock 'em over with my ear-piercing delivery, I knocked 'em over with the tacky taffeta and frilly skirts my Gangy sewed for me. *Good Lord,* you say, *who's Gangy?* Well, that's the name I gave my precious grandmother, who was the real voice of the voiceless Grand Pop Link.

It was pure fun for me to do little pirouettes and cartwheels across living room floors. It was sheer bliss to discover multiple, innovative ways I could irritate everybody. Be comforted if you have a child like me. She (or he) will grow up very fast, and she (or he) just might be a serious performer or preacher one day!

This tSUEnami-Sue-Lee-whirlwind charged on through the decades but now operates on a new paradigm. An outgoing and hyper-excitable little girl is now an adult whose joy it is to turn the word "fun" into a beneficial ministry of humor, music and sacred sarcasm. I laugh when I think how God uses the very traits that others consider precocious or, worse, intolerable! And now I use it all to bring Jesus to life for others. Thanks be to Him!

Let's just blame it all on hurricane Connie. She's the one who blew into town, flooding streets, wiping out power lines, and setting my poor mother into fast labor. Even from the start, I couldn't be contained.

A tSUEnami Warning

The forces of nature and acts of God have no explanation or warning. My personal tsunamic desire is to symbolically knock out a few self-righteous religious poles, wipe out women's ministry power struggles and egos, and shake up a few hallowed hierarchy establishments. I am driven to make His presence known. A few of my ministry friends choose to stay in the safe zone. I don't blame them. It's easier to not make waves. But that's not for me. I do more than push the envelope; I'll dance around it as I hand it back to you.

When a real tsunami washes ashore, it always leaves debris in the aftermath. But I can tell you this: I'm not the first, or the last, to heal from a wipeout of devastation. I thank God everyday for the recovery of and call on my life.

Rev. John Hamercheck, my former pastor, would often shake his head at my antics. He wasn't too keen about my healthy disrespect and lack of pulpit etiquette. Rev. John was the first to say, "Have Sue Duffield come to your church. She'll not only comfort the afflicted, but she'll afflict the comfortable."

True.

So, how are you doing?

- Have you survived a personal tsunami of your own?
- Have you been someone else's personal tsunami?
- Have you raised any roofs lately?
- And what about the debris you left behind?

Questions that might be best to avoid? Since this is my book, I want to help you out here. When you're thinking about the impact you want to make in the world:

Be diverse.
Be broad-minded.
Be uncategorized.
Be out-of-the-box.
Be extraneous.
Be supplemental.
Be an outlier.
Be beyond the norm.
And especially, be a living, breathing Jesus to a bored and spiritually dead world.

Don't worry about labels. Don't waste your time looking to be card-catalogued, promoted, or categorized like some level of hurricane intensity. Be shockingly you; making your own waves.

A tSUEnami prayer:

"God, take me and shake me down to my foundation. Help me know the difference between when You're opening and closing doors. And even if I refuse to understand the swinging of the door in both directions, help me always trust You. Heal my doubt in You. Help me not be surprised by the enormity of Your quaking needed in my heart. And help me to hold on tightly to the grace you give even when the waves surround me. Help me also to be aware of those who are struggling to survive their own storm. Restore unto us, Jesus, the joy of Your salvation."

~

Yeun wakes me by tapping my shoulder and says it's time. The pilots are closing the doors of this big beluga whale Airbus 770. They close in a methodical computer-like Star Trek synchrony. We'll be taking off momentarily and flying at mega-altitudes, rising high above many storms. And the clicking sound of the doors say to me, *That's one door I don't have to worry about.* I am safe and secure. The doors are closed, and that's a good thing on a plane.

Yes, closed doors can be very, very good for you.

CHAPTER TWO

"SUErreal"

The seatmate who enlightened me on the Anne Murray exchange, is Mei Chen. She's en route to Kuala Lumpur, too. I'm so excited to find out she also has a twelve-hour layover in Seoul. We compare travel notes and flights, realizing we're on the same exact flight pattern all the way from Atlanta to KL. This probably thrills me way more than it does Mei, but she shows signs she just might enjoy my peculiar motherly company. She asks if I have any Band-Aids, aspirin or dental floss. I laugh to myself, and think, "*What does she think I am, an American drug store?*" And, of course, I have every one of those items.

Mei is a wide-smiling Malaysian who happens to be a student at a pharmaceutical school in Ohio. I'm so impressed with her. She speaks Korean, Mandarin, and English. By now she's figured out that the only additional language I speak is *laughinese*. Her cute little teasing jabs point me to the medicinal benefits of getting off sugar. She's the diet police, eyeing the snacks and food fragments in my carry-on.

"So, Mei, what happens when Yeun and her sisterly flight attendants offer us those famous almond-puff *saccharinafied* Korean pastries? I hear they're rolled in powdered sugar. Hmm, Mei? How healthy is that? Hmm?"

"You may take small bite; leave rest on plate." Mei is chiding me as she adjusts her seat belt. "It quite acceptable. You no have to eat all."

"Doesn't sound like much fun to me, leaving delectables on a dish. In America we wipe our plates clean, maybe even use tongue to lick the plate; especially dessert."

Mei frowns. "In America, too much medicine and too much sugar. You people not just wipe off you plate, you wipe out you body."

She does this quirky cockeyed grin and goes back to reading the chapter on Opiates in her big black pharmaceutical book. No wonder she's on this kick about drugs and sugar. We converse in agreement that the sweet stuff is bad for the body and is unfortunately found in most processed foods. Mei still lectures me while she reads.

"Too much sugar affect everything, Missasue."

She has no idea how right she is.

I love speaking and singing at the "Chocolate & Chuckles" women's events around the country that I do with churches. I'm sure you think I just roll up to the cocoa trough and dip my body into Hershey's Chocolate syrup. And I'm not above it. But for all the weekends of women's events and dessert-athons I'm a part of, I'm better off hanging out with the fruit, cheese, and toothpicks.

Before a comedy concert one night, I drove all day from New York to Pennsylvania and had no time to grab protein or anything healthy. When I got to the Chocolate & Chuckles venue, I couldn't resist. The hall was gloriously decorated in rich colors of cocoa brown and atomic orange, with an acre-long buffet of chocolate heaven! Every table and station offered an abundance of homemade, bakery-made, and I-don't-know-and-I-don't-care-who-made chocolate desserts. I grabbed a plate, loaded it up, and shouted, "Oh well, here we go! I surely don't want to disappoint anyone . . . "

Like a kid on sugar-overload, it wasn't long before I felt the surge of sugar high and craziness hit me. "This isn't good," I thought. Seriously, not good. Couple that with the fact that I'd been on the road for ten days in a row, and it made for one dangerous and disastrous combination.

The time came for the performance to begin, and, in some respects, it already had. It sounds SUErreal, but a church full of women, giddy and laughing from their own blood sugar blasts, sealed my doom—and I hadn't even hit the stage yet. *An audience that laughs at everything is like a drug to me.* Buzzing, I waited for the women's ministry leader to introduce me. From the podium she mentioned that childcare and a nursery were available for the few women who had brought children. She also suggested that women should feel free to go to the buffet of chocolate any time throughout the program. Oh boy.

The first twenty minutes on stage were a struggle for me. My timing was way off, and I was feeling a little lightheaded. I blamed the sugar coma and the long travel. Right in front of me on the first row sat a sweet young mom with her highly energized toddler in tow. When I say he was all over the place, he was, *literally,* All. Over. The. Place. But, being a professional, I kept doing my thing, while she struggled to keep him quiet. Here's how it went:

Public me: (Telling a funny story)

Private me: *She must have completely ignored the childcare announcement.*

Public me: (Singing to connect punch line to poignant truth) "Everyone needs forgiveness, the kindness of a Savior . . ."

Private me: *Maybe she's one of those new waves of moms who don't trust church nurseries.*

All this chaos continued, inside my head and out, as the little tyke was crawling up and down his mommy's leg, and then—and then . . . he smacked her in the face and proceeded to scream for about ten minutes straight.

Private me: *Smacked her?! In. The. Face!*

There was an obvious strain in the room. Women were giving me looks like, *Do something,*

Sue. Some of them shook their heads in disgust. It was clearly very uncomfortable for all involved. I was hoping either the pastor's wife or women's ministry leader would intervene and gather the toddler and take him to the nursery, but, you know, I get it. Sometimes you just aren't sure what to do or how far you can go with someone's children.

I just kept singing, dancing, telling dumb stories, and trying my best to rise above it all. Finally, the distressed mom reached her breaking point. She grabbed her toddler and rushed out to the hallway, but not without a fight from the tiny tyrant. He was squirming and squinting, waving and yelling. "Don't spank me, Mommeee! Don't spank MEEEE!"

As I stood watching, the darndest thing happened: the microphone in my hand transformed into a ground attendant's neon flashlight directing her to the back as though I was leading an airplane back to the gate.

Now, the women seemed instantly relieved the little menace had evaporated. We were one in our relief, and with absolutely no restraint or filter on my tongue, I shouted to the recovering audience. "You know? If that was me when I was a little kid in church, my mother would've hauled my **a**** to the parking lot."

No one moved. The only thing that broke the silence was the picture of Jesus on the back wall of the sanctuary unhooking and rocking from side to side. And, to be clear, the utterance that escaped from my mouth was not a cleaned-up version." I said THE word.

Those wonderful, religious women looked at me in total surprise, reminding me of the Christmas caroler figurines, the ones with their hands folded and mouths wide open. After a few seconds that lasted weeks, my trusted new girlfriends erupted into applause, pointing at me and laughing in hysterics. I assumed by their response that they weren't as much in favor of what I had just said, but more in shock that "SUErreal" blurted out what they were all probably thinking anyway.

I froze, thinking *I cannot believe I just said the "a-double-scribble" word! Out loud! In church!* And maybe it wasn't just that I had said THE A-word, but how I'd said it. After a few beats, I took a deep breath and spoke into my mic: "Forgive me, Father, for I have sinned. Can I just blame the demon of sugary chocolate that got the best of me?"

On my way out the door that night, a teenager grabbed my hand and said, "Don't worry, Ms. Sue. We all know 'ass' is in the Bible. Thanks for being real." I warmly thanked her, to which she added, "It like totally cracked me up. I about fell off my chair! And I didn't even want to come to this thing tonight to begin with. Shoot, I sure wish my friends were here! I texted them all and said, 'You'd love this speaker. She got everybody's attention, all right!'"

Being real IS surreal sometimes. It's risky and can be downright embarrassing.

Yes, a** is in the Bible. And mine is typically in a mess of trouble.

For instance, I've experienced a few wardrobe malfunctions while performing, long before that phrase was made popular by a mishap at a Superbowl halftime show by a certain pop sensation.

In the days of long skirts and thin chenille fabric I walked across the stage with an abundance of spotlights behind me. I'll never forget the horror on my mother's face at one of my first concerts. Sitting in the front row, she put her hand to her mouth, gasping. I didn't wear a slip under my flimsy chenille skirt.

Did you know *chenille* in French means *caterpillar*? That's about right, because the fabric was creeping into every crevice of my posterior.

The stage lighting behind me was about as revealing as an x-ray machine, detailing all of my everything in full silhouette view. Not a good day. My mother rushed out of the auditorium, drove all the way home and came back later with my slip. I was good to go for the second half of the program. I think this could have been where my husband, Jeff, my forever keyboardist, and I became known as the "Christian Captain and Chenille."

On another occasion, a very important supportive undergarment strap broke while I was singing on stage. I heard the snap before I felt it pop my skin. It happened so fast, but in slow motion, the strap sprang loose and hit me in the chin! There is no way people on the front row did not hear and see it, too. There was only one way for me to react: I quickly went to prayer.

"Everyone, close your eyes and bow your heads," I said to the bewildered crowd in my most spirit-moved voice. "NOW. No one looking around— " I sounded extremely urgent and very spiritual.

Obeying my command, they dropped their heads and closed their eyes. Surveying the rows for complete participation, I stealthily collected the strap, which had somehow made its way from undergarment to outer garment (hanging around my neck!) and stuffed it back inside my blouse— all the while still praying, mind you. Finally, thinking I had it all under control I realized that the strap had worked its way out of my blouse through to my left short sleeve. In my panic I must have over-stuffed it back into my blouse, because it was now hanging and dangling completely on the outside under my arm. How's that for a mental image?

Those were early days of speaking and singing when I was afraid of unexpected interruptions. If things like this happen today, you better believe I just go right along with it and make it part of my prop and comedy routine. How it might go now: "Oh look, a wayward bra strap. Isn't that the way we are? We want to see what all the fun is and leave the safety of our proper place. I like to call this story the parable of the prodigal underwear. A reckless, wayward strap awol from its duty and security. Only this time it's forcefully returned and put into its original "place," after the grab and reprimand of its owner, both joyfully relieved and repentantly received."

I didn't exactly use much wardrobe discretion back in the seventies either. I'd proudly wear short skirts, tube tops, and tight-fitted clothing. Why not? I had the body to pull it off. Today, I wouldn't be caught dead in a short skirt or tube top; and not because I have some sort of clothesline religion. It's just that I don't care to expose everything and blind everyone!

I arrived at a hotel one weekend realizing as I was unpacking that I had forgotten the most essential supportive undergarment: my good Sunday bra. All women have that one faithful truss; the one we just know always works. I had packed one of those flattening camisoles, but that would never work getting dressed up for Sunday. And of course, my hotel was conveniently located in the middle of nowhere. I had two choices: Walmart or Dollar Store.

I have no problem with discount store clothing. But in reality, you pretty much get what you pay for. I found an off-brand, black, full-figured slingshot-looking thing for about eight dollars and thought, *"Well, let's just give this a shot."* I laughed at myself with the implication of those words. Oh, it worked, all right. *Sling* and *shot* - very prophetic.

Pointing my way through the crowd, I looked like an Egyptian princess in full armor with two pyramids. I kept thinking of songs I would **not** sing that day, like "Love Lift Us Up Where We Belong" or "Love Lifted Me." I feared poking an eye out if I bent down to pray for someone. I also reminded myself not to say the word **point** at any point in my message. No references to *Point* of Grace or Power*Point* either. And, no hugs. We wouldn't want any full frontal injuries.

Let's talk shoes. I'm a huge fan of Naturalizer shoes. It's not unlike me to buy several versions and heights of high heels. I own two pairs of navy blue Naturalizer pumps; one medium high heel and the other, low heel. So when I packed for an event, I grabbed a pair out of my closet and headed on my merry way to Boston.

I don't generally put on my high heels until I actually get to the stage. I bring an extra bag just for that purpose. I wear my casual shoes to the church then change into my heels right before I go on the platform.

At this Boston event, I slipped into my heels just offstage, as usual. After being introduced I began to walk across the stage—with a noticeable limp. I looked down to find, on my left foot, a navy blue *low* heel pump, and on my right foot, a navy blue *high* heel pump. By the time I got to the microphone, the crowd was on to me. It was pretty obvious to them what was going on, being women.

The first words out of my mouth as I pointed down to my feet were, "And here's the crazy part. I have a pair just like this at home."

The place went nuts. To make the most of the moment, I limp-walked back and forth on the stage, modeling this new look in exaggerated Carol Burnett fashion. Up, down, up, down, on and on until the laughter eventually subsided. My wardrobe oops made me my own warm-up act.

So here's my reality check. The more I live life in a holistic, self-deprecating, and not-so-serious way, the more I have a shot at clearing the air and opening the path to this unusual and underestimated gospel. It's Jesus who heals the unreal to become real. Strange, bizarre, unusual, and weird people have a place in the kingdom of God, too. In fact, "they" are the VIPs of the Kingdom. And if God can use my scattered craziness, as surreal as it sounds, He can surely use yours.

"Dear Friend, listen well to my words; tune your ears to my voice. Keep my message in plain view at all times. Concentrate. Learn it by heart! Those who discover these words live, really live; body and soul, they're bursting with health." (Proverbs 4:20-22 MSG)

A SUErreal prayer:
"God, help me to know that the biggest and best challenge will be the fight to be real. The sustaining power of Your grace in my life through your son Jesus gives me no other alternative than to be totally authentic. My greatest asset is not talent or gifting. My greatest gift is the exceptional truth that You live through me each day. There is no alternative. Guard my mouth and correct me from busyness and distraction. Help me to keep it real."

~

"Ms. Sue? I think Yeun wants you attention," Mei says, tapping my arm. I look up to see Yeun staring me down, holding a familiar object.

"This not good," Yeun says, shaking a rather tattered Dunkin' Donuts sack. "Contraband, Missasue. This yours?"

I act surprised. Mostly I'm thinking *Missasue* is just too adorable.

"Nope. Not mine. Where you find?" I don't mean to emulate them, and I'm certainly not one to mock, but my English slides into *Engrish* in spite of myself.

"Under you seat," she frowns as she wags the bag. "It fell into aisle way."

"Maybe I did have something like that in my backpack. I can't remember . . . " I give Yeun a sheepish look as I turn and wink at Mei. The Dunkin' Donuts kiosk was my last point of passage from Atlanta to Seoul. Gathering donuts and leaving their crumbs of evidence everywhere was probably my Hansel and Gretel way of navigating new territory.

"Ahh, no wonder you smell like donut, Missasue," Yeun says, "'cause you sit on glazed one."

Guilty. I sit on donut. And as surreal as it sounds, I also sit on the complete truth that God is right next to me no matter the mishaps or frenzy that happens everyday. It's a sweet life.

CHAPTER THREE

"ConSUEcrate"

I feel sorry for babies on overseas flights. I catch the eye of a little guy about three rows ahead. He's been restless the last hour or so. I can relate. I'm restless, too. His mother, Ms. Clueless-ta I'll call her, is pretty much letting him overtake the plane. Yeun must be sleeping or hiding in the Korean Airliner's secret quarters. She is nowhere to be found.

We have a brand new flight attendant this evening. Shen is her name, and she is fast at work trying to comfort Mr. Squealmeister, while pacifying the passengers. I watch her ask the baby's mom if she can hold him. Shen leans in to pick up the little disgruntled boy, and as soon as she does he settles right down. He gazes into her face and smiles. Shen is my new best friend. Shen is a pro. A few around me smile, too, nodding their heads while gesturing in a silent air-clapping motion. I nominate Shen to be this little boy's personal attendant for the rest of the flight.

Now that it's back to the jet engine hum, I close my eyes and doze off. I'm falling in and out of consciousness, thinking about a dinner I sang and spoke at a few years back for Child Evangelism Fellowship. The beautiful ballroom of the Registry Hotel was filled with unfamiliar supporters. You might find this surprising, but I'm not the best small talk person in a formal setting. It's weird: everything I do is so public. But those kinds of events stress me out. A room filled with suits, noxious perfumes, and monotone chitchat just about does me in. My husband Jeff shines in this kind of environment. I'd rather go hide in the corner of the room or hallway to just watch and observe.

That day, though, God knew I needed a subtle kick in the head. The CEF conference wasn't about my comfort; it was about the dedication and mission outreach that men and women devote to teach the gospel to children worldwide. And if there's one way to get my attention and pull me out of a corner, just start talking about reaching children with the gospel of Jesus Christ.

I knew little about CEF at that point of the briefing, but when one of the keynote speakers began to talk about Good News Clubs around the world, I dropped my spoon to my plate. The slow motion clang startled everyone at the table. In unison, they all turned their heads from the speaker to me. My body might have been sitting in that velvet chair of the Registry Ballroom, but immediately my mind flashed back to summer days on Dixie Drive, in New Jersey.

It was 1961. When that first little postcard announcement arrived in our mailbox saying, "Good News Club is Coming to Your Neighborhood!" I ran into the house, skinned knees and all, waving the card in the air and shouting, "I'm goin'! I'm goin'!" The postcard was placed on the refrigerator underneath one of my mother's insurance agency magnets. The countdown to our little street's children's gathering was on.

The summer Bible Club series was usually weeklong and was always held in the backyard of the house between Regional and Dixie Drive. My brother, Dave, and I could not wait to go. It was like an oasis of "not really school" in the summer. Many of the kids on our block went because we were bored and needed something to do. Friends, stories, songs, games, and snacks, hurray!

We learned about Jesus, the flannelgraph man. He tested the power of the flannel board in the wind. We sang songs like, "Stop, and let me tell you, what the Lord has done for me." We memorized Bible verses, and of course we always looked forward to the snacks, like peanut butter crackers, Tollhouse cookies, or Rice Krispy Treats. There was nothing better in the world.

At that CEF conference, my Sixties summer mind-movie played the whole time the keynote speaker was presenting. I wasn't really listening, just reminiscing. But then, he said something life-changing:

You know, there might be someone in this room right now who's been influenced by the gospel of Jesus through a summer Bible club. Our Good News Clubs were quite popular in the Sixties and Seventies. Every conference, we meet adults who as children found their way into someone's backyard to hear Bible stories. Is there anyone here that was influenced by a Good News Club?

Without hesitation, I shoved my hand into the air. It wasn't my adult hand, but my six-year-old hand, waving back and forth. All I needed at that point was a Rice Krispy Treat.

"I'm one," I said out loud, as people turned around, looking at me.

When you're raised in a Christian family and church is your entire life, it's hard to know exactly where or when you made a decision to follow Jesus. But that day I knew. It all came back to me right there at that round table. I gave God back His sacred space in my heart, the space He created in me for Him when I was in Mrs. Wylie's backyard. It was then I knew I would conSUEcrate my life to Him forever.

It was a very emotional moment for me. I might have been sitting in a ballroom, in that velvety chair, in my nicest black dress, as an adult, but my short little legs were swinging on the backyard swing underneath Mrs. Wylie's canopy in my mind.

After the session concluded and my tablemates were filing out of the room, someone tapped me on the shoulder and said, "Sue, our CEF President would like you to share your story about your Good News Club experience at the next session. Can you do that?"

Oh my. *"This will be so unrehearsed,"* I thought. Now, that in itself was funny. My whole career as a speaker/singer for over forty years has thrived on the unrehearsed. But my backyard experience would be a new old story to the ears in that ballroom. It also would be a brand new confession, from my lips to my own ears.

I motioned to the banquet staff, asking one of the waiters in a whisper, "You guys wouldn't happen to have Rice Krispy Treats, would you?" You can imagine the look I got considering we just were served fresh pecan-crusted Chilean Sea Bass, garlic roasted asparagus, and red raspberry white chocolate cheesecake for dessert. Very adult foods. Somehow, though, they located a Rice Krispy Treat, and with that little manila-colored sticky confection in hand, I made my way to the platform. I shared about this Jesus, the flannelgraph man, and how I consecrated my life to him at a Good News Club on Dixie Drive.

The child in me attracts other children. A little boy, maybe the only one in attendance at this very adult affair, stared at me the whole time I was speaking. He couldn't have been more than five years old. So intent was his attention that I was determined to take some time to find out who he was and what he was thinking about while I was talking.

I made my way down from the stage, put my hand out as if to shake hands, and he jumped into my arms. Overcome with emotion, I whispered in his ear, "You have no idea how you have made my day. What a special young man you are! You made it pretty easy for me to tell this story today!"

I was all emotional, the tears melting my mascara, when he said, "Ms. Sue?"

I replied in a goofy, whimpering voice, "Yes, my little friend?"

He paused, put his head back, and said, "Your breath is reeallly bad!" Then he wiggled himself out of my arms and skipped away.

Scoundrel.

In my recent retreat-speaking years, I have encountered something new. More young moms are bringing their infants and small toddlers to these events. I'm not a proponent of bringing young children to women's retreats, only because I know that as a mom you'll be spending more time in the hallways than in the sessions. I also know that the squabbles, the crying, and the disruptions can offend the other attendees who paid money to get away and learn. I don't blame them. It's also hard for a speaker to work with all the distractions.

The other side of the story goes like this: Many of these young moms wouldn't be able to come without bringing their children—some by choice, because some feel no one is qualified to watch their children—others by the fact that anyone they would even remotely trust to watch their children for the weekend are probably already here with them at the retreat.

At one such retreat, Courtney, a busy little two-year-old, was quite a handful. Her mom, whom I loved instantly, was spending more time in the foyer and her hotel room than in any of the sessions. She had all three of her children with her at this "retreat." Her life was in crisis mode, and many around her knew this. I was not aware. At least not right away.

Courtney was in the back of the ballroom just being a typical two-year-old. I have to admit I was very close to frustration myself, knowing that the other women were as fatigued with the interruption as I was. I was oh-so-close to asking if someone wouldn't mind taking her out to the foyer. But instead, I just started to sing.

I'm forgiven, because You were forsaken . . . I'm accepted, You were condemned. I'm alive and well, Your spirit is within me, because You died and rose again . . .

I watched as Courtney separated herself from her mother. The child walked slowly up the center aisle toward me. I kept singing and got down on my knees to sing to her face-to-face.

She didn't move.

I stared into those pretty blue eyes while at the same time stroked her hair and tiny shoulders. It was a tender, divine, consecrated interruption. A sacred stop. The Holy Spirit had an agenda, and it was up to me to flow with it or lose it. Courtney, her mom, her family, and their situation needed a major miracle. It was in that anointed pause that I believe God showed me something I needed to be shown. He showed me how to quit.

- To quit trying to make things work on my own.
- To quit trying to force things to happen.
- To quit being the manipulator and orchestrator and let God direct the symphony.
- To quit being a controlling adult.
- And to never forget my childlike hunger for God.

That's what being consecrated is all about. Being solely (and souly) His.

Courtney and I sang "Jesus Loves Me" together. That singular moment of the retreat will never be duplicated. I'm not sure how effective my pre-planned topic was for that weekend, but I do know we were all sure that something special had happened to us. I know that all 150 women, plus one little one, were deeply moved by the Spirit of God.

I'm still not a proponent of bringing kids to women's retreats, but I've got to say, that sweet moment paints a superb picture of what the cutout Jesus on that flannel board would do. To stop and be interrupted by children is to see the hand of Jesus at work.

Yes, interruptions are a real pain, aren't they? Wouldn't it be amazing if we all allowed ourselves to flow with Godly peace even when life is totally out of control? Giving God sacred permission to barge in is to be forever consecrated to Him. The child in me says, "Yes. Because . . . Jesus. Loves. Me."

Driving the Pennsylvania Turnpike one Mother's Day away from my own kids, I randomly interviewed travelers at the rest area. To every woman I would come into contact with, I said, "Happy Mother's Day". Their reactions were priceless:

Me: Happy Mother's Day.
Woman: You talkin' to me? OH, I guess you are! (laughs) Well, thank you, then. I'm kinda sick . . . "

Me: Happy Mother's Day.
Woman: Wow, that sure is nice. Thank you! My kids don't live around here, so thanks a lot!

Me: Happy Mother's Day.
Woman: I don't have kids.
Me: That's okay.
Woman: But I do have ovaries, so I guess there's hope, right?!
Me (laughing): Yes! There's always hope!
Woman: I just have to find the right testicles.
[Yes, she did say that!]

Me: Happy Mother's Day.
Man: You're kidding, right?
[I just wanted to see what a man would say!]

Me: Happy Mother's Day.

Woman (with her adult child with special needs in a wheelchair): Thank you, it's the best. And my girl is the best!

Me: Yes, she is. Can I hug her?

Woman: Yes, but be careful, she might not let go!!

[I hugged her, and for sure, it took a few minutes to pry myself away.]

Me: She's got a great momma. Thanks for being the best example yet of being a devoted mom.

Woman: Hey, we do what we gotta do. We love our kids no matter what.

I'm never disappointed when I interview people. From all walks of life, these women (and one interesting man) just crack me up! Most people, if given the chance, show their true colors in less than a second.

My mother's consecration to God was over the top. I miss her so much. You would have loved Naomi Beatty. She was everything I am not. Petite, dainty, structured, and disciplined. She did instill in me the blessing of mothering and setting her children free. I'm so glad my kids give me hope that somewhere along the line I did something right. And if you don't have children of your own, whether or not by choice, you have no less as a person, as a woman. It's never too late to spiritually adopt children, taking them by the hand, mentoring and loving them like they're your own.

I love being a woman with great potential to change the world. Let's do this. Bless a child today, whether you're genetically attached or not. Pour the investment of love into them. Even in pain, hardship, or loss, wrap your arms around a child or teenager or an adult "baby", and lavish them with hope for their future. It's a very economical way to give a gift, yet so valuable and life-changing.

My mother used to say, "Mother's Day is a lot like Father's Day, except the presents are a LOT more expensive!" Justifiably so, in her case. She deserved the best.

I had to work through some challenges growing up on Dixie Drive. As I grew older, I'm sad to say I didn't always live up to the consecrated life I wanted to have. Some bad choices as a young girl made for no perfection here, that is for sure. But my flannelgraph Jesus still leaps off that board today. He's alive and living in my heart.

Jesus called out to a child and stood him in the middle of the room, saying,

"I'm telling you, once and for all, that unless you return to square one and start over like children, you're not even going to get a look at the kingdom, let alone get in. Whoever becomes simple and elemental again, like this child, will rank high in God's kingdom. What's more, when you receive the childlike on my account, it's the same as receiving me." (Matthew 18:2–5, MSG)

A conSUEcrated prayer:

"God, all Your works will praise You. And all Your saints will praise You. I will speak of the glory of Your kingdom. I consecrate my life to you, in child-like faith. Wake me everyday, with the majesty of your grace and forgiveness. Awaken my heart for this earthly life, to be more like You. Thank you for your son, Jesus, who leaps off a flannelgraph board and into my heart."

~

As I stir from a nap on this flight, I still see Shen walking the aisles with Mr. Squealmeister. She has much more patience than I. I open one of the three books I brought with me. A leather-bound, worn out, teal-colored book with "Naomi Beatty" embossed in gold on the front. My mother's Bible. It is a risk bringing this fragile Bible on the trip, but I had to. On one of the first blank pages inside, my mother wrote, "Pray for Carrie in Malaysia". I think to myself, *"I will, Mom. And I'm doing more than just praying for her. I'm going to see her and the rescued girls she has helped to rehabilitate, and I'm taking you with me."*

"You're with me, Mom," I say softly under my breath. "You're with me."

CHAPTER FOUR

"SUErround"

Keiko Matsui, an amazing jazz pianist, is playing her magic in my headphones. I found her while scanning all the satellite radio channels on this Korean Airliner. I cannot tell you how euphoric this is for me. I'm surrounded by smells, sounds, and tastes that are everything SEAsian. Most of the three hundred or so passengers are Korean, and I love being the minority.

Mei leans in to me and whispers, "The warm towels coming. The warm towels coming!" And sure enough, as soon as she says this, another flight attendant I haven't yet met hands me a warm, moist towel with silver tongs from a silver bowl.

"What do I do with this?" I ask Mei.

"You wash your face and hands. And don't forget to put on slippers. Take shoes off. We are supposed to sleep now. And when we wake, we eat Korean sweet cake. Much like American donut, but way better." Mei puts her head back and laughs. She knows she's got me wrapped around her little finger. I so want to capture all of this on video, but instead I write in my journal. As I write, I'm thinking about how to stay connected with Mei, my new, and hopefully lifetime, friend.

A few years ago, my best friend Dawn and I were Skyping and made quite a scene at Detroit Metro Airport. She was at her house in western Michigan, and I at a seat in Terminal A. We were both howling in laughter at our screens thinking back to the time she tripped and fell in the mud on a rainy Sunday morning.

Dawn was wearing a beautiful, black Kasper suit she'd just bought at Macy's. Running through the parking lot to escape the torrential downpour, we made an impulsive decision and attempted to jump over a flowerbed near the church entrance.

Key word, *attempt*. Dawn fell flat in the mud and I was stumbling behind her. Well, I just lost it. Thankfully she wasn't hurt, but I was immobilized and bent over with crippling laughter.

It was as if I'd been shot with a stun gun. I couldn't breathe, I was laughing so hard. I was trying to help her up, but every time I grabbed her hand, I collapsed in a weakened, crazed state. Drenched Presbyterians dashed right by us into the dry shelter of the church. Knotted up in hysterics, we could barely make it inside the church. We dashed to the ladies room and tried scrubbing mud off her suit and my shoes, but mud was e-v-e-r-y-w-h-e-r-e! In her hair, behind her ears, even in her underwear. Wet paper towels only made it worse. Dawn wasn't laughing nearly as much as I was at this point, but it was quite the scene. Women who had just arrived at church surrounded the ladies room, snickering as they witnessed this muddy prelude to the service.

Morning worship was soon to start, and I was the singer/speaker for the day. All that laughter was a spurt of healing joy for me. How in the world do you gather your composure after an experience like that? You can't. Or at least, I couldn't!

I have had many experiences of conSUEming belly laughter. Once, on a very turbulent plane ride I drank one too many cups of water. I needed to use the lavatory in the worst way. The plane was packed. It was only a matter of time before the *seatbelts fastened* light would be illuminated. I had the window seat in a row just behind first class, and of course, had to bother the young couple next to me to let me out. The lavatory at the front of the plane was not working, so I had to weave to the one at the back of the plane.

I was wearing a pretty little summer dress. This is rare. Most times when traveling, I wear jeans or comfy clothes, but my daughter, Annie, who is my fashion police, insists I should dress a little more feminine and age appropriate. The turbulence was getting worse, so I rushed to do what I needed to. I entered the potty cubicle. As soon as I sat down the pilot said, "All passengers PLEASE report to their seats, immediately. Flight attendants, secure your positions."

Great. I quickly jumped up, burst out of the door and fast trotted the e-n-t-i-r-e length of the plane...with my dress stuck in my granny panties! Not one person stopped me to inform me. I guess they figured with all the turbulence, a crazed woman exposing her rear end was the least of their worries. I got to my row, and rather than ask the couple to get up out of their seats to let me in, I motioned to them and said, "Don't worry. Just sit. I'll crawl over you."

Yes, that's what I did. They sat there while I hobbled in front of them ('scuse, me, pardon me, 'scuse me, pardon me) with my exposed you-know-what in their faces. It is when I collapsed in my seat that I thought, *"Dear God, why is this leather seat so cold?"*

I knew—that sensation is unmistakable—that my dress was stuck in my underwear. The gal next to me said, flippantly, "I was gonna say something to you, but I didn't know what to say." I stared straight ahead and answered back, "By the time I got to you, it was a little too late anyway".

I bent over to get my purse, and when I did, everything came tumbling out of it—gum, lipstick, Kleenex pack, Tums; scattering everywhere. My business card holder landed over by the man sitting across the aisle. He picked it up, and the cards came flying out. He gathered them up and held one in his hand to read it. He looked at me, and said, "Wow, are you in show business?"

(Long pause) I exhaled and said, "Yes. As of today. I just showed my business."

It's not surprising to me anymore that the women I meet, especially over the recent series of LOL (Laugh Out Loud, Live Out Loud, 'Cause He's Lord of Lords-themed retreat), Girls Night Out, and Chuckles & Chocolate events I do, have incredibly gripping faith stories. Stories that aren't very neat and clean, from atheists to crack addicts and former prostitutes on parole. I feel like Dorothy when she said to Toto, "We're not in Kansas anymore".

Kansas for me, in this metaphor, used to mean well-groomed, shiny-faced, picture-perfect June Cleaver women who do church, have church, and live church. The churchy women. You know, the squeaky clean, non-messy, religious ladies' get-togethers that rank right up there with Martha Stewart hospitality goodness. That's what it used to be.

Until . . .

I started praying for revival and outreach like never before. I started to take note that through the promotion of comedy and humor, women show up. Some come without any pew-sitting background at all. No church history. Hope, healing laughter, and encouragement are quite the draw, and I'm totally SUErrounding myself with all of this.

I grip the left hand of a thirteen-year-old girl who's been cutting herself but wants the words to my crazy acronym-texting song, *LOL*, while at the same time I grasp the right hand of an eighty-nine year old woman who says out loud, "My heart has been heavy for so long. I needed to laugh SO badly tonight. Thank you."

I see a lot of joy and fun in women's events around the world, but I also see distance, anxiety, hurt, and lack of trust, too. Laughter can and will actually expose more about who you are than you may realize.

Readying myself for a recent LOL retreat, I wrote in my journal:

> *What you laugh about defines you.*
> *What you cry about refines you.*
> *What you pray about assigns you.*
> *What you give to God aligns you.*

Laugh. Cry. Pray. Give. Four power-packed action verbs that will keep you centered. Surround yourself with friends who love to laugh. Surround yourself with friends who cry with you. Surround yourself with prayer partners, especially the interceding ones who pray "without ceasing" with fervor, everyday—in the middle of the night, whenever prompted, at all times of the day. Surround yourself with giving, generous people. Hang with those who feed you, not bleed you.

Don't go one day without scheduling some sort of fun. Did you know that we are spiritually wired to smile? You were designed to enjoy a good belly laugh and see the humor in things. My husband, Jeff, knows I can't go one day without teasing him. It brings me such joy! He says potato, I say po-tah-to; I say granola bar, he says Snickers. I needle him constantly about his peculiarly sub-par and "no greens" diet. He says I eat bark. I say he's content to drink sweet tea and eat M & M Peanuts his whole life. We joke constantly about food. I'll say to him, "Would you like to taste this pimento mousse hummus filled with shallots and dill?" He'll say, "I'd rather eat the package." It's therapeutic, and it sure keeps things fresh around our house.

Our adult children, David and Annie, have the humor gene. It's inherent. And the thing they find the most fun these days is to make fun of their mother. My kids tell me I never really "listen" to them; or I filter it when I DO listen. They do get my attention when they call me "Susie!" Whatever. I taught them well!

The smartest, easiest way to care for your own wellbeing is to surround yourself with those who have a positive approach to life. Lean in, learn, and receive from those who understand holy humor and live life to the fullest everyday. Contagious laughter in abundance in your soul opens your heart. It's like a reboot or restart on a computer. And if you laugh so hard you can't catch your breath, the medicinal benefits abound. It can actually restore and cleanse your body. It's just like God to make something so trivial as laughter to have power like medicine.

Laughter opens the door*, and it's the most covert evangelistic tool out there. It works every time. Take my new atheist friend, who returned to hear me for the second time in two years. She approached me at the end of a recent concert.

"Hi Sue," she said. "I didn't agree with all your religious talk or what you sang about tonight."

I didn't flinch or act surprised. I smiled and said, "That's okay. You came! And I wouldn't think you would agree with me, as I probably wouldn't agree with you at your meetings."

"My sister made me come the first time, but I came back on my own this time", she said. I'm sure she expected a typical, judgy response.

"That's really cool, Mary," I say.

Mary wasn't engaging in much eye contact, but that was okay. She continued. "I liked it when you sang the Oldies, and I really liked the comedy and stuff, but the Jesus part—not so much."

I put my hand out to shake hands and she grabbed it. "Thanks, Mary, for being honest. This same Jesus that sings and speaks through me during the Oldies and all that crazy humor is also the same Jesus who cares very deeply for you. And since He lives inside me, He's got your hand right now."

She looked down at my hand, then up at me, and smiled and slowly turned away. I don't know what happened in her heart, but I surrounded her with Jesus in that moment.

One of my favorite Facebook posts was from a woman attending a church here in Nashville. When she "checked in" and wrote a status update, she inadvertently checked in to the Hooter's restaurant that was right across from her church. She wrote, "In His Presence - at Hooters!" Her friend's comment under the status update was just as good: "G-i-r-l, you better cross that street!"

I believe God gave me a communicable funny disease. (But my strain is more of a *dizzy-ease!*) It's infectious, transmittable, and very influential. I'm always in search of true to life stories with a spontaneous, kid-like frolic (not that I really have to search—they tend to find me!). Laughter is the supernatural drug that costs nothing, but is priceless to a sick body or soul. People are drawn to happy people. I grew up in a home where laughter was the norm, and it is my intent to keep the generational blessing alive and well.

For all my social media friends and experts out there who post on a regular basis, let me help you with something: Don't be so super-spiritual. Try to ease off the judgment a little. Don't express hatred through sarcasm. *Do* invite others into your conversation. Applaud, praise, and comment on posts that are worthy of your approval. Be communicable in the best of ways. Revel in your shortcomings. You never look better to the world than when you are real, vulnerable, and not taking yourself so seriously.

Sophie, a little friend I met at an event her mom brought her to, doesn't smile much. She'll turn six years old soon, and she's missing some teeth. Last time I saw her, I said, "Oh Dear Sophie, your new teeth will grow fast. You'll draw more people when you smile!"

She looked at me, dumbfounded, and said, "If I smile, I can draw people? I can't draw people too good. I can draw trees and horses better. You wanna draw with me?"

That cracked me up! She picked up a brown crayon, and drew a picture of me. When she handed it to me, I chuckled because I looked like a horse! She smiled, big time, and said, "You told me to draw you, and I drew you, right Ms. Sue?"

Yes, baby girl, you drew me, all right. Love the teeth . . .

Atmosphere and engagement with any audience starts with you, whether online or in person. The truth is, I don't make the distinction or consider a difference between being real in person, in public, or online. It's so easy to hide behind the computer screen or even live a life of make-believe. But, eventually, you'll be found out. Sooner or later, our posts, tweets, and status updates reflect what we're really about. It doesn't take long for our true personalities to seep through the Internet. I have to unfollow some people, purely because their posts irritate me or don't speak life to me. It's so much healthier to surround yourself with people who are consistent in their vision and their positive outlook on life.

I purposely post ridiculous stories about myself just to get responses. I want to see who's paying attention. The other day I posted this on Facebook:

> *I have tried over 20+ deodorants in the past several months. All to combat this change-of-life hormonal desperation to not smell like used kitty litter. Well, I finally found Tom's Natural Long-lasting Apricot deodorant. Awesome. Now I smell like apricot-scented used kitty litter." #thoughtyouwouldenjoythis*

As you can imagine, the comments rolled in. I laugh because some of them took me seriously, prescribing all kinds of remedies. But most of them posted "LOL" and "laughing over here".

I cannot stress to you how critical it is to **resist the temptation to be negative online** at any time. Give and share the healing power of your hilarious moments, encoded with the magnet of the gospel. Draw them in. Then, when their ears and hearts are open wide, you have the open air space to deliver your message. Just love them, for goodness sake!

Psalm 109:30-31 MSG nails it:

"My mouth's full of great praise for God, I'm singing his hallelujahs SURROUNDed (emphasis mine) by crowds, For He's always at hand to take the side of the needy, to rescue a life from the unjust judge."

" . . . surrounded by crowds . . . " It sure sounds to me like crowds will follow those who sing HIS hallelujahs and those whose mouths are full of great praise. I wish we could grasp this concept. We attract others more when we get rid of our own pious presence and envelop others with HIS presence.

A "SUErround" prayer:

"Father God, help me to be a laughter-light to a critically dark world. Engage me to be more like You, so when I am with others they will see Your presence. Surround your Holy Spirit in my home

and my family. Help me with my attitude and servitude. Instruct my mouth to tell of your righteousness. Thank you, God, for turning my mourning into dancing."

~

Sure enough, like clockwork, this aromatic puffy Korean pastry delight arrives right under my nose like some glorious olfactory alarm clock. I open my eyes and behold this glorious presentation of fresh raspberries and sugary pastry on a china plate.

Mei motions to me, as if I need coercing, to try it. Then she says, "Trust me, Missasue. You forget ALL about American donut when you teeth into that." I chuckle to myself at her English. "When you teeth into that..." Love it.

*Laughter Opens The Door, song written by Sue Duffield on her "LOL" album

CHAPTER FIVE

"SUEtencils"

We're flying at least 40,000 feet over the upper Aleutian Islands by now. Yeun and her team of attendants suddenly appear from behind that secret curtain. They're passing out chopsticks to each wearied passenger. Oh boy, this ain't good.

"Sue, you need chopstick for fish and lice?"

What? I so want to "help" Yeun with her pronunciation, but I know if I do I may have a bowl on my head.

"No thanks, Yeun, I prefer American fork." I peer up over my glasses to see what kind of reaction I get.

"Missasue? You no quite daring, are you? No curry, no chopstick?"

"No, but I quite hungry." I laugh.

"You no be Korean if you no like fish and lice."

"I love fish, but I like it be more dead—with no eyeball glaring at me. And I'd like the rice not to move like lice."

"Sue, you make fun with me, no? I have eyeball on you," Yeun says, winking with one eye.

I'm sure she does. Rice, lice, fish with eyeballs—they're all looking at me.

"Just be thankful and eat," I whisper to myself.

Yeun is quick. I take the plastic fork she hands me. It's wrapped in a warm towelette. I await the arrival of the *fish and lice*, as Yeun so endearingly says. Mei is engrossed in her rice bowl and books, but then she glances at my mother's Bible in the pouch of the seat in front of me.

"I can read?" She points at the teal-colored Bible.

"Of course, Mei. It's my book of choice." I carefully place it in Mei's hands. "I live by it, or at least I try to."

And right there begins the journey of opening hearts on spiritual things; several hours of storytelling into this flight. I was waiting for her to ask. She looks at the engraved name on the outside. *Naomi Beatty.* She runs her finger across my mother's name and says, "It like she come with you, no?"

I don't know why, but Mei's question stays with me for hours. I always dreamed of taking an overseas journey with my mother. We sure enjoyed lots of trips to East Coast beaches, campgrounds, and events, but we never crossed the ocean together. I guess in a way, Mei is right. Her legacy is right here with me. Her Bible, with her scribbled handwriting and outlined notes, is definitely close, both on this plane and in my heart.

Besides my Bible, my SUEtensils of choice today are chopsticks and a fork. Growing up on Dixie Drive, we never seemed to be able to hold onto important gadgets, utensils, or kitchen devices. They tended to disappear. I laugh to myself remembering the inquiring questions my mother would pronounce, to nobody, as if into the air . . .

"Where in the world is the slotted spoon?"

"What happened to the good scissors?"

"I think we lost the church key." (That's an old-timer's description of a can or bottle opener.)

"How come the only clean forks left are the pie forks?"

"Do you think we can have one good knife in this house . . . one that's sharp??"

"Where's the Scotch tape?"

For generations, and maybe this is indicative of how some things get passed down, the simplest little kitchen utensil or household tool just seemed to walk off with the dish that ran away with the spoon. Now, in my own house, I can never seem to find a flathead screwdriver. Plenty of rubber bands on doorknobs, but never a Phillips head when you need it. The other day I spent an hour just looking for a hammer.

A hairbrush, though, was a household item I never lost track of, growing up. If you're a singer, it is a given that at some point in your lifetime, your round hairbrush was a pretend microphone. Mine surely was. Long hours of performing in front of a mirror, backdropped by my avocado green walls, framed me with quite the Seventies flare. We were living the retro Seventies long before it was chic.

In one hand, I held my round brush from the W.T. Grant store; in the other hand, I gripped my avocado green Princess Phone with the extra long, eighteen feet of curly knotted cord. Man, that cord got quite a workout, bending around corners, wearing the paint off the woodwork, wrapping itself around end tables, and choking a cat or two. I could sit on the stair steps some fifteen feet away from the dock of the phone and talk to my boyfriend Jeff until the wee hours of the morning. So freeing and miraculous, never dreaming one day we'd all carry personal handheld computers and small cordless phones in our pockets.

But the SUEtensils, as I look back, held certain significance in my "hand-held-objects" life. Just about everything meaningful to me, for my sport or entertainment, came from an object I'd hold in my hand.

My dad bought my first condenser microphone from Radio Shack. It was a really big deal. No one in church was holding a microphone to sing from yet. To be properly reverent, a microphone must stay on the stand or podium, no handheld microphones were even allowed in some churches. It was much too worldly looking, like a nightclub singer or something. All the more the reason to do it, as far as I was concerned. This little pencil-like mic was a newfound wonder, a whole new world to sing into and hear my voice amplified. Later, God would open doors for me to do radio and use another kind of microphone (the 'net!) to connect with an invisible yet real audience—all tools to send forth my message.

When our kids were in grade school, through to junior high, I was an announcer and DJ for WNRK radio in Delaware. This was a great perk for them, considering all the free stuff I'd get from promotional advertisers. They loved hearing my voice in the mornings, while their dad was trying to jam cereal down their throats so they could catch the bus. David and Annie weren't too happy when I left the station, so they suggested I just set up my own microphone and broadcast from the kitchen . . . then, send dad out for the free stuff.

The day I walked away from radio, I remember feeling so lost. Those first few months after leaving the station were quite an adjustment. No platform to speak anymore, and surely no outlet to broadcast my craziness. I pretended to do radio on Annie's plastic toy microphone for therapy, which my kids thought was hilarious. Eventually I would find another SUEtensil; another technological medium to broadcast my craziness and wild adventures. It would take my daughter Annie to teach me. My smart kid taught me how to use a smart phone, and then encouraged me to sign up on Facebook, Instagram, Twitter, and also to do some blogging. Kids are great teachers!

A tennis racket, a basketball, and a microphone defined my life as a teen. I was good enough to make the teams in high school but not good enough to make sports a career. Juggling these three items was enough to keep me off the streets and out of trouble. The cool thing in high school was bringing my "One Way" Living Bible to class everyday, which would become the most important SUEtensil of all. Of course that had to be avocado green too, so it fit quite nicely with my fashion statement.

When I was about nine, we had our windows and doors wide open one summer night and my implement of choice for the evening was a red fly swatter. My mother gestured to me, pointed to the wall with it, and said, "Get that mosquito over there!"

I got up, and I swatted, and missed. Then I swatted again. And missed again.

My mother, the armchair mosquito swatter, said, "You're missing it! Get closer."

Obedient daughter that I was, I stood on the couch and swatted again, still missing it. Then, in my frustration, a phrase (in my head, picking up the language of my neighbor kids, to be cool, maybe?) I hadn't planned to SAY came flying out of my mouth. "I can't get the *dang* thing!" (and we all know I didn't say "dang".)

The holy hush and shivering silence in the room was so steamy it scorched the mosquito to the floor. My brother skedaddled to the kitchen. He knew what was coming. My four-feet-nine-inch, powerhouse of a mom rose from the couch, grabbed me by the shoulders, and shook me, saying, "What. In. The. World. Did. You. Just. SAY?"

It's kind of blurry now, truthfully, but the only thing I recall next is sitting in my room curled up in a fetal position. I was grounded, big time, stripped of all my SUEtensils. No Princess phone, no tennis racquet, no basketball, no microphone, no transistor radio, no nothin'. I was in some serious trouble. No amount of talking my way out of it would work this time. And the same mosquito that played dead downstairs, or one of his cousins, found his way up to my room, laughing and buzzing around my head.

Now that I'm a grown woman, my life is pretty much dictated by my iPhone. My calendar, social media, books, contacts, music, and connection to people are all in there. I feel like Siri is my mother. I sent a text to Jeff today using Siri that she translated as, "I'm at Planet Firmness."

Firmness? Prophetic, I hope. Yes, that's what Siri said. Firmness.

I say aloud, "No Siri, Planet Fitness."

She says, "Did you say Planter Bitterness?"

"No, Siri, Planet FITNESS!"

Siri says, "Did you mean to say "Plant Fastener? . . . Plane Finesse?"

I'm dying by now.

Finally, Siri tries again with the best autocorrect of all. "I'm sorry, did you say Plantar Fasciitis?"

Sometimes I feel so ancient when it comes to this fast-paced instant communication journey we're all on. It kind of goes hand in hand with the ever-changing ministry God sets before me. Staying both relevant to this generation while

54

never loosening my grip on my retro foundational teaching pretty much throws me into the perpetual spin of reinvention. I may long for the days of my Princess phone, but I wouldn't trade it one bit for the rapid advances of technology. It more effectively connects me to people, and people are my ministry.

Understanding Jeremiah, the prophet, and his specific calling (without technology) is crucial not just to understanding the whole of the book of Jeremiah, but our own personal calling and ministry for the kingdom of God. Jeremiah undertook the battle for God's Word at a time when almost no one wanted to hear it. These days, they'd probably just "unfollow" or "unfriend" him.

I especially love Jeremiah 1:5 from The Message. *"Before I shaped you in the womb, I knew all about you. Before you saw the light of day, I had holy plans for you: A prophet to the nations—that's what I had in mind for you."*

Jeremiah is just one of a handful of prophets among thousands of false ones. Many of the so-called leaders of his day were making money and enamored with fame, counterfeiting and twisting their authority. Sounds eerily and culturally familiar, doesn't it? Those in authority of the day don't want to recognize it and the majority of so-called spiritual leaders are making money and building their fake kingdoms. Doesn't sound much like "holy plans," does it?

There are four very distinct actions in this verse:

If God is texting you today, He doesn't say, "I framed you." He says, "I formed you". We are shaped for His purpose.

God would never text, "I knock you." He says, "I know you". We are individually identified for His purpose.

God needs no autocorrect. He never says, "I confiscated you". He says, "I consecrated you". We are separated from the world's ways for His purpose.

God would never text you, saying, "I have appalled you." He very distinctly says, "I have appointed you". We are *specifically* called for His purpose. And that, by the way, is in His official Text.

Wouldn't it be great to set your mind on God's autocorrect? You know, the days that come when you feel so unqualified or insignificant that you can't even speak (or text) with purpose? God takes our feeble, filthy words and makes the ultimate autocorrect through the giving of His Son, Jesus. The greatest words from the cross happened when Jesus said, "It is finished." satan (undeserving of a capital "s") no longer had the tools to defeat Jesus. And satan has no tools or power over us either!

A SUEtencil Prayer

Praise You, God, for Your handiwork and breathing words, the Living Word that jumps into my heart from Your life-text! Thank you Lord, for the abundant tools you give me to spread the gospel. Thank you for correction. Thank for you for reminding me that the instruments you give are just that: instruments—to be used for your kingdom. Keep me close to you and keep my mouth in check. May your Holy Spirit be my greatest guide.

~

Yeun and the crew are gathering what's left of the plates of fish and rice. The trays, linens, and trash disappear. Looks like most of my flight-mates have eaten all their dinner. And, surprisingly, I have too. It didn't taste all that good, truthfully, but I look down at my glass plate and catch a glint of my reflection. For a moment I forget that Mei is beside me, and I'm pretending like I'm looking into a mirror. I'm trying to use a fork to get a piece of fish out from between my teeth. Mei leans into the plate, sees her reflection too and says, "You look like me, Missa Sue?"

We laugh. And then I hug her.

I say, "For sure I look like you, Mei; you have fish in your teeth too!"

I don't know what is happening at this point, but a surge is pulsing through my heart. Mei is making her way into my soul space, and I am quite comfortable with that. It's surprising to me how much I care for her in such a short period of time. I just feel so connected to her, this stranger-friend. I don't dare say a word. I'm afraid I'll ruin it. But I know that something special is happening between my new friend and me. And Jesus is right in the middle of it all.

"Did you save chopstick, Missasue?"

"I sure did," I say, fumbling through my bag of stuff.

"You might need them where you going." Mei leans her head against the window.

"Where may I and Mei be going?" I laugh as I fumble through that question.

"We go to great Korean kitchen gadget and utensil store in Seoul. They have best sushi restaurant there, but you bring you own chopstick." She clacks her pair of plane-issued chopsticks together in my face. Mei actually twirls the chopsticks through her fingers like a ninja warrior using his hands with swords! "But you okay if you bring you American plastic fork, missasue."

Mei makes me laugh, again.

CHAPTER SIX

"SUEspicious"

My head can't get around the fact that we can fly for over fourteen hours and not stop for fuel. This amazing ship with wings is supplied with just about anything required to sustain human life. About an hour before our descent, I make the mistake of walking to the front of the plane to catch a glimpse of Business Class. There's definitely a whole lot more room for your wiggle. Mei tells me that the sleeping cubicles in First Class are even more depressing to view, especially for us regular poor people.

Mei whispers from the side of her mouth. "It can cost up to 11,000 round trip dollar for First Class."

"You are kidding me? Who can afford that?"

"Rich Korean businessman, that who," she says. "One man I met make trip from Seoul to Atlanta four to five time a month. He always fly First Class. I ask him adopt me!" She chuckles.

"I don't think you should talk to strangers, and you should never ask a man you don't know to adopt you, Mei." The wiggling I do this time in my seat isn't just because of fatigue, but it's because I'm a little riled at Mei's statement.

"Well, I talk to you, and you stranger." She has a point.

"Yes, but I'm not a man. I'm a mom. And I have kids your age, so I can surely look after you." When I say those words to her, I get that same warm fuzzy feeling inside. I repeat to myself, *I really can look after you, Mei.*

Mei adds, "When we land, we take tour through Seoul. I take you to wok restaurant downtown. We have twelve-hour layover in Seoul before we fly to KL. You like?"

"Oh Mei, I would love that! But is it safe downtown?"

"Seoul is safest town you ever know. Even better than New Jersey. You feel like little girl again. I take care of you."

After years of world travel, I get a little suspicious of dark parking lots. Long desolate hallways in hotels and spooky rest areas along the interstates get to me, too. When I was younger, stuff like that didn't bother me much. But now I take special note of unusual surroundings or potentially anomalous people. I know I don't live on Dixie Drive anymore, and I have to negotiate that trusting feeling of how I was raised. It's not that I'm naïve, but I just think somewhere along the line I matured into the possession of a healthy suspicion of things.

I was very SUEspicious when my dad said that it would be okay to use a fresh water fishing pole one summer to reel in flounder on Cape May

Point beach. "But dad, won't people make fun of me with this bulky fresh water pole, fishin' with it in the salt water?" The black pole with the oversized bulb, which rewinds the fishing line back into the spool, gets all stiff and stuck with salt. Freshwater doesn't do this, but saltwater to a freshwater pole is like grinding grains of salt deposits. I can still hear that sound in my head. And my little hands could barely wind it. But you better believe it, no one would ever know. I was determined to be a strong girl, and show up the boys.

Even back then, I had great concern about what people thought of me. Later when metal braces and pimples would befall my appearance, I worried more. I didn't smile as much, and I covered my face with flesh-colored acne cream. Those were awkward days. And don't you know I hauled in more flounder off that point than anyone that day. Frustrated fishermen beside me, with their expensive lures and premium, saltwater-resistant poles became very suspicious of me. They'd look in my bucket, see about six trophy flounder, and walk away shaking their heads. This was a major accomplishment. *I'm a girl! And I'm a darn good fisherman!*

"What kind of bait you usin'?" one man asked.

"She's just using worms!" My brother bragged, dancing around the bucket. "She's just using wor-orms! Ha! And she don't got the right fishing rod!"

Beach time with my little brother Dave goes down as some of my most favorite childhood moments. We probably have more pictures of us on beaches than anywhere else in our family photo albums. No, I didn't have the acceptable pole. And no, I didn't have the right bait. All I know is, I got the abundant result and will gloat over this fish story for a lifetime.

I'm resistant sometimes, and a little suspicious of what the Spirit might be up to, when I write new songs that might be way out of the box. But I have to trust God and give Him my creativity, which He gave me in the first place. You may not have all the goods, talent, or the perfect vehicle to get your word out, but if you never take risks with the gifts God instills in you, you'll never be entrusted with new gifts or new resources.

I grew up with a bunch of kids in the Sixties and Seventies who went to church, but most of them didn't grow up Pentecostal like I did. They weren't privy to all the religious-sounding talk spoken as a first language in my world back then. Once, I brought my friend Lois to a Sunday service. She looked a little suspicious when I addressed everyone as *Brother* Smith, *Sister* Jones, or *Uncle* John. After the introductions, she pulled me aside and said, "Sue, I know it's a small church and everything, but, wow—are you related to *everybody in here?*"

I heard a story about a new young Christian raised on the streets, asking his pastor if he could participate in the Communion service. The young man begged to say something prior to the elements being distributed to the congregation. Apprehensive and suspicious, the pastor slowly handed the Communion cup to the young man. In his exuberance and joy over his new walk with Christ, the young man lifted the chalice and shouted, "You see this cup? This blood's for you!" Then he raised both hands high, pointed to the ceiling and yelled, "You're the M-A-N!"

When Mike, a Jewish friend of mine, came to a concert at a Pentecostal church, it was his very first time to be present in an atmosphere of exuberant praise and worship. When the music started and people began raising their hands in praise to God, Mike couldn't figure out why so many people had questions. Afterward, over Cokes at a burger joint, he said, "They just kept raising their hands the whole time, obviously having questions or comments about the music. Why didn't anyone acknowledge them?" God love him.

Years ago, back when my children were young, I would not have been as prepared as I am today for opportunities to speak at secular or beyond-the-church-wall events. To assume that everyone will understand or comprehend the Christian-ese way of speaking is a real mistake. Today I am challenged and held accountable to keep from getting caught up in the rhetoric of dated language and religious expression. If I say, "I am saved," for example, some will ask, "Saved?? From what?"

Here's how I let go of Christian-ese talk and share more of Christian–ease.

1. The proliferation of the spiritual attitude that "I've always said it this way" is a real guarantee you'll be ineffective. It's nothing more than a habit. Be willing to examine what words you use to communicate about the gospel. For example, instead of saying, "God is good all of the time" (which He is), simply ask, "Is God real to you?" or "How can I pray for you?" or even, "Who is God to you?"

2. Words like *redeemed*, *saved*, *sanctified*, and *blessed* are incredibly endearing and meaningful to those of us who grew up hearing those words, but to this generation, our words probably sound like the droning teacher on the Charlie Brown cartoon series: "Wah, wah, wah." Speak words that connect, without a bunch of religious talk. Relate your story of what being a Christ-follower means to you.

3. Jesus, the Master Communicator, told parables using secular examples from His own society and culture, conveying and sometimes baffling His listeners and followers. Some heard it; some did not. Some "got it" and were radically changed. Even Jesus said, "I did not come to destroy the law of the Prophets, but to fulfill it." (Matthew 5:17) He was misunderstood. Many people would walk away, skeptical and full of suspicion. But one thing is for sure, He offered hope to the hopeless, whether they totally understood or not.

"The Message is as true among you today as when you first heard it. It doesn't diminish or weaken over time. It's the same all over the world. The Message bears fruit and gets larger and stronger, just as it has in you. From the very first day you heard and recognized the truth of what God is doing, you've been hungry for more." (Colossians 1:5,6 MSG)

Maybe my suspicion about life is this: I am so hungry for more. I am curious about this living gospel of Jesus. I am always searching for answers and desiring to camp in that continuous eager-to-know state. Maybe that's why I never tire of asking questions.

My heart leaps off this page to think that you may be searching and hungering, too. I pray you'll become sincerely suspicious, in a good way, of the life-changing gospel. Try Jesus, ask Him, and question Him. The Living Word will never fail you.

I mistrust a husband or wife who rarely talks about his or her family. Maybe that's because my parents spoiled us, always talking about their kids. It's like a silent test I give to people I meet. Spending time with musicians, ministers, and prominent people is a perk to this life I've led. But over an initial conversation, I'm a bit suspicious about a man who doesn't talk about his wife or kids in the first ten minutes. I know I sound like I'm judging here, but I've been right more than wrong in my assessment: Men or women who rarely speak positively about their spouses or their families rarely have good relationships *with* them. And I put myself through that filter too, knowing that whatever's in my heart blurts out of my mouth. I have no unspoken thought. I carry my kids, my husband, my family, and my dearest friends in my heart and soul. There is plenty of room for all of them.

Get really suspicious of your self-talk, too. You are valued, loved, esteemed and worth dying for. If you follow Jesus' words and still struggle with putting yourself down, there's no room for that. Don't ever forget that your heavenly Father always talks about His kids with joy and delight.

A SUEspicous prayer

As it is written in Jeremiah 10: 6, 7, (AMP) "There is none like You, O Lord. You are great, and great is Your mighty and powerful name. Who would not fear You, O King of the nations? For it is appropriate and it is Your due! For among all the wise men of the nations and in all their kingdoms, there is none like You."

Help me Lord, to never be in doubt or in suspicion of Your great Name. Help me not to focus merely on questioning, but help my unbelief. Help me to trust You, for You are worthy.

~

As you can probably imagine, Mei has had her fill of Duffield stories by now, though she has been a rapt and captive audience these many hours. I've had fourteen hours to jabber, brag, and make her feel like she's part of my family. She was shocked to hear I married at nineteen.

"Oh, way too young, Missasue," she said.

She especially loves the stories of my kids. "I wish to meet them someday, Missasue. I feel like I know them."

On our descent into Seoul, Mei gets a little fidgety. She leans over and whispers in my ear. "Missasue, I have something important to tell you. Come here close—" She pauses, looks from side to side, and says, "You need mint. Your breath bad!" Then she throws her head back and laughs out loud.

Yeun is walking with her cast of Korean beauties up and down the aisles preparing everyone for our entry into Seoul Incheon International Airport. She smiles at me and says, "Now Sue, you have flat butt like all rest of us Koreans since you sit on it for fourteen hour!" She chuckles and winks at me as she saunters by. "And don't forget, Missasue. Korean Airline the best. You tell everybody."

As Yeun walks away from me, I mimic her in a playful way, with my eyes squinting and lips protruding, saying, "Korean Airline the best . . . Korean Airline the best!"

Yeun puts her hand through her hair, takes out her pretty blue hibiscus-shaped plastic barrette, and hands it to me. "You keep, Missasue. This help you remember."

I hesitate. No American flight attendant has ever offered me a gift.

"You do not need be suspicious of Korean generosity," Yeun says with a genuine smile. "We giving people."

I may not see her or her team of lovelies again, but I'll never forget her charm and hospitality. I hold on to that barrette all the way until we land, that little blue charm now a cherished memento.

CHAPTER SEVEN

"SUEture"

Mei is so excited about upcoming adventures during our long layover in Seoul. She's writing a checklist of places we need to see and things we have to do. We're descending through layers of dense clouds when Mei starts to sing, "Ain't no stopping us now, we on the move . . ."

How does Mei know that McFadden and Whitehead song? Talk about surreal.

"RAIN no stoppin' us now, we on the move, Missasue!"

And she is even doing that Travolta disco move with her hand. I watch with wonder.

"We run through raindrops or take bike," Mei says, with all her youth and optimism.

"YOU run and take bike, Mei. I take photo. And how do you know that song?!"

"You have much to learn, Missasue." Mei is still bouncing her head to the music in her mind. "Philly sound big in Malaysia."

Hmmm.

The plane makes a smooth touchdown. I'm anxious to get off, but I also want to stay put.

There were too many sacred and fun moments in those fourteen hours. I didn't get much sleep, but no worries. The promise of a Seoul adventure stimulates a surge of adrenaline through this weary body.

The captain makes an announcement in Korean, and most of the passengers are going, "Ugh, oh no."

"What??" I look at Mei, and she takes her hand and covers my mouth while she tilts her head to listen. I'm very impatient because I want to know what's going on. Just as she starts to interpret for me, the captain interrupts in English.

"We sorry to inform you," the captain says in an accent slightly less thick than Yeun's. "You must stay seated. We have a very sick passenger on board. We wait until medic come with ambulance."

Fourteen hours in the sky, and now we sit. For how long? *A passenger is sick? Aren't there like twenty exit doors on this plane? Ugh.*

So we sit. And then we sit some more. We sit for almost an hour. I busy myself with journaling. I distract myself with inventory of my stuff, gathering tissues and wrappers to throw away. I put my head back and sigh. Such a long wait!

Mei says, "You Christian, Sue, why you no pray for passenger? Then maybe we get off quicker."

Ouch. She's right. I was moaning about being inconvenienced, all the while a poor man has had to have an emergency tracheotomy, right on the floor about nine rows ahead of me. Not to mention the sutures he'll need in his throat.

"Sutures." Does that word not just make you hurt? The medical definition of the word suture is: a *stitch or row of stitches holding together the edges of a wound or a surgical incision*. Mei is putting her head down on the tray table, and all I'm doing is becoming more fidgety in my impatience, wondering why we can't exit through the other doors using the other aisle. I'm acting so American right now. Most of the other passengers are silent, even reverent. I'm mad because I just lost an hour in Seoul.

Part of my problem is I really like to fix things. My son, David, has always had a knack for fixing stuff. Even as a little boy he would take toys and motors apart just so he could figure out how they work and then put them all back together again. While Jeff, Annie, and I couldn't care less about machines, engines, or anything mechanical, God gave us David to take care of all that for us.

But the kinds of things I want to fix are, well, people's attitudes. It's in my blood. My Gangy Link was that way. She, without any training or education, had a knack for fixing people. Accepting their failures and imperfections, mending their hearts, and understanding their depression. She did it all by her intoxicating way of loving them to pieces. And even if you didn't want to be fixed, she'd fix you anyway.

But the older I get, I realize I can't fix people. My SUEturizing tendencies have been a real headache and heartache over the years. *You* *mean to tell me that most people don't **want** to be fixed?* Yeah, that's pretty much what I'm sayin'.

The first year we lived in Nashville, when I was fifty-something, I went flying off the front of my bicycle handlebars at about 20 MPH. My front tire lodged itself in the side of the curb as I was turning off the street. It flipped me forward about ten feet into the air. Half my body landed on the pavement and the other half on the grass. First the thud, then the "ughhhh."

Fortunately, the most padded parts of my fifty-ish frame hit the sidewalk. I picked grass out of my teeth for hours after. I lay there moaning in a half-daze. "God, please send a Good Samaritan, hopefully someone old or female, or a doctor or something, who can help me get up. If it must be a man, please make him average looking." Every bone in my rib cage felt compressed.

Out of nowhere, a man ran toward me. Full of drawl, he said, "Ma'am? Ma'am! Are you awll wraht?" He was a very muscular southern young man in athletic attire.

I looked up and sighed. God, The Master Comedian, had sent me Matt Damon. Well, not actually Damon, but you understand. He picked me up with one fell swoop, hefting me in one arm while rolling my bent up bike with his other arm. He carried me all the way back to my house over a block away, making conversation to make me feel less awkward. He told me he's a musician and has worked with Kenny Chesney, and a few other bands we've all heard on country radio and seen at the CMAs.

Jeff met us at the front door and couldn't believe his eyes. A big, brawny, scantily clad man was lugging his wife into the house. Wearing his little Nike running shorts, no shirt, and those weird looking Five Finger Minimalist running shoes, this angel-in-disguise lowered me slowly onto the sofa. Now that's service.

While I was dying on the couch, Jeff and the Good (looking) Samaritan started talking musician-speak. For an hour. Or more. Did I mention I was croaking? *I need sutures, people!* The worst was the bruising. It took weeks to heal. The only benefit of the fiasco was that it would give me yet another great story to share.

I needed a few sutures earlier in our marriage, too. We lost our first pregnancy. The pain of letting my body do what it needed to do to naturally miscarry was a war. My OB/GYN assured me that first time pregnancies can sometimes happen this way. No young woman wants to hear that, but at eleven weeks, my hopes and dreams of a baby were lost.

All kinds of people wanted to fix me, mend me, and encourage me. I don't blame them. They meant well. I'd want to fix their pain, too. I still knew that God had a plan for me. Three friends in three separate scenarios all quoted Jeremiah 29:11 to me that day.

Three friends. Three times. The same scripture. All in one day. God wanted my attention. *"For I know the plans I have for you, declares the Lord. Plans to prosper and not harm you. Plans to give you hope and a future."*

A year after my miscarriage, I sang at a church where a woman came up to me and said, "You're pregnant. And you're going to have a boy." *OK. Here we go again.* We asked the pastor what he knew of this woman, and he confirmed her solid reputation, and said she wouldn't typically say anything prophetic or off the wall. The next day, I bought a pregnancy test. It was positive, and David Scott was born seven months later.

Friends and family had been praying for me. Too many prayers maybe, because fifteen months after that, Anne Kathryn was born! Two babies in just over two years. A gal from Canada told me she was praying that God would bless my womb. I sent her a note saying, "Okay, you can quit praying now. We are done."

I sang at a women's conference, taking both my babies with me. The theme of the event was "Come Expecting!" I kid you not. *Plans to give you hope and a future.* Pretty amazing. As I walked into the ballroom, the leader of the event looked down in the double stroller and said, "Now, Sue, which one is *Hope* and which one is *Future*?!" Funny girl.

Our backyard pool is surrounded by Bradford Pear trees. It tests my salvation trying to keep it clean and clear of leaves. Most people think they want a pool, until they measure the upkeep against the amount of times they actually do any plunging. The kind of pool I want someday is in a gated adult community where old people just sit around and complain about their hemorrhoids and homeowner's fees. Our first summer in the house, we discovered a leak and a hole in the pool liner the size of a pencil eraser. I bought a pool repair kit with epoxy, sealant, several patches, and sixty pages of "how to." I decided to take on the repair myself.

With all the necessary accoutrements spread out beside the steps of the pool, I plunged in, fully clothed. (Don't ask me why. If I were swimming I might have put on a swimsuit, but it was autumn, and this was work, so I wore work clothes!) I slowly submerged a cinderblock wrapped with rope, and tied the other end to the bottom of one leg of my jeans. *Yeah, go ahead and laugh.*

It was October and fifty degrees outside. The water was actually warmer than the air, but not by much. I was freezing but knew I had little time to get this job done. With my hands above water, I smeared epoxy on the latex patch, folded it in half, held my breath, and submerged myself to the bottom of the pool. Without realizing it, some of the epoxy had drizzled off the patch and down my hand. Which was not a problem until I scratched my head. Now I've got epoxy in my hair and I can't remove my hand off my head without pulling out my hair. I hold my breath, submerge again, find the hole in the liner, unfold the patch under the water and smack it on the hole. It sticks! I come up for breath, then go down again to see if it has staying power, and it does!

Would I be smart enough to have someone guiding me along, to oversee, to protect, to witness? Oh no. Not me. I'm SUEture-girl! When I go down the second time, my hair gets stuck to the extra epoxy around the hole. I'm gulping for air at the same time while my jeans are tied to the cinder block holding me under. This really should have been on video. I pull my hair from the patch area, then pull off my jeans under water. I grab the side of the pool and pull myself up on to the deck. I do a slo-mo squish walk for ten feet to the backdoor - with no clothes on except my drenched sweat shirt. *See? I can fix things!*

The epoxy in my hair had to be cut out. And when I pull the jeans tied to the cinderblock out of the water with a pool pole, that's when I lost it and started laughing uncontrollably. No one will ever believe this.

Another definition of the word suture is: *to unite; to bring together.* I guess I really am a SUEture. Nothing brings me more joy and happiness then to see the knitting together of friends and family. It's not always easy, and it sure can hurt sometimes, but the connection of bringing two separate and distinct entities together makes me dance.

God always puts people in our paths for a reason. Helping to solve problems or even throw around ideas for others is such a high for me. Zig Ziglar said that those who solve the biggest problems get the biggest payoff. I'm still waiting for that big payoff, but I do feel called to bring people together, to see the hand of God heal as I listen to what He says to do. *See? I can fix things.*

Nobody fixes and heals like God does. He will turn His heart toward you when you turn your heart toward the needs of others. Pray for your friends. Pray for Christians around the world and watch how God answers your prayers as you lift the prayers for the righteous.

One night after traveling to speak at an event in Springfield, MA, I was so tired, but the women who flew me in for their event wanted to go out. My SUEture tendency of bringing people together was in full force. I told Kelly, "I'm really divided as to whether I should go out or not. My right brain says, 'Yay, Sue, go have fun!" And at the same time my left brain says, "Go home, you fool. You're too tired!" Kelly said, (and what a great line), "Well, fight amongst yourself and let us know." LOL.

On an early morning back in the Eighties, I am speedily driving to my morning shift at WNRK Radio in Delaware. I stop quickly on the side of the road to pick up the local paper from a coin-operated newspaper box. Pulling over to the side of the road and frivolously jumping out of the van with two quarters in hand, I think I set the gearshift to P (for Park). But stumbling out to the curb, my two-ton van begins a backward drift. *I must have put it in reverse instead of park.* Great.

I run back and jump in the van with half my body in and the other half out. I try to reach my right foot on the brake pedal. Good instincts. Stopping it or slowing it down while hopping and grabbing the driver's side door was futile. I could NOT stop the rolling beast. Take note: If you're ever in this situation, the one thing that WILL stop a moving driverless vehicle is a stationary telephone pole. It works every time.

The door and I are hanging on for dear life. The pole catches the open door bending it forwards (or backwards, really) in slow motion. The door bends all the way around forward and I become jostled between the pole and the side of the van. I try to pry myself free enough to leap around into the van to completely stop it. It stops. I jump in the driver's seat and attempt to bend the door back to a closed position but there's no way. It's almost 5:45 a.m., and I need to be on the air in fifteen minutes. Picture this: I can't budge the bent-around door and I drive the busy rush hour highway with my right hand on the steering wheel and my left hand gripping the door which is w-i-d-e open, facing the wrong direction!

My husband is never going to believe this, AND he's going to kill me. When I get to the station I have one minute to spare before linking up satellites, grabbing the program log, and saying, "Good morning, Oldies Radio!" I call my husband during a commercial break.

"Umm..something strange happened to the driver's door of the van, honey..."

Strange and *honey*; two words I never use in the same sentence. It's a dead giveaway to Jeff that this ain't good. His reaction was priceless. I was in some big trouble, but I survived. After several hundred dollars later everything was back to normal. Well, it's never normal. That not-so-euphoric experience was quite the conversation joke for the guys at North East Body Shop in Wilmington for a while. Until Jeff had his own "come-to-Jesus-meeting" with a vehicle and a pole at an ice cream stand. But that's another story.

A SUEture prayer

Thank you, God, for comforting me in all my afflictions, so that I, too, may comfort others in their affliction. Bless you, Father, for repairing and stitching me up when I do stupid things. Protect me, God, when bad decisions surmount and tough times take their toll. Surely goodness and mercy will follow me all the days of my life, so that I may dwell in Your life house forever. Amen.

~

I grab Mei's hand as we deplane, finally, and head into Incheon Airport. What an exquisite high-tech wonder. I'm staring up at the gorgeous kites and architecture while Mei is pulling me, saying, "Let's bolt, Missasue, we have much do today. We go to Chojun Textile and Quilt Art Museum, then Gyeongbokgung Palace. You will like!"

I'm in stitches just trying to pronounce these places.

CHAPTER EIGHT

"SUErrender"

Not only is Mei a master of navigation through massive Incheon, she also has experience with bus routes touring Seoul and outlying areas. And apart from studying at a pharmaceutical school, she really loves classical music. "I take you to sushi place where they play my kind music," she says. I'm wondering where the sushi place fits in with the wok visit, but I've surrendered to her lead. I'm all hers for the day. We drop off our bags at a security locker space and head on to our adventure.

On the bus ride to downtown, Mei confides, "My father and mother never leave Malaysia. It hard for them, when I go far away. It like they no understand. But I smart. I find my way."

I felt the same way, when I left home at eighteen and married at nineteen. Oh, I knew my mother was proud of me for pursuing a career in music, but I think there were times she wished I would've stayed in South Jersey, worked for DuPont, had a bunch of kids and forgot this traveling-singing circus.

"I had to leave Kuala Lumpur for a while. Too many problem, Missasue."

I pause and wait to see if she will continue. "Why?"

Outside our windows, I see a more industrialized city than I had expected. Lots of construction and roadwork with hard–to–navigate streets. It is a cloudy day, with sprinkling rain, but I don't care. As far as I am concerned, it is a sunny day with an interruption of glimmering rain-shine.

"My dad's friend who work on our house, he got too friendly with me." She looks at me with her big brown eyes. "He touch me where he should not touch."

I've suspected all along that God had me sit next to Mei for this reason alone, and I hope for an opportunity to ease her pain. I don't know at this point if she'll offer me any more details. I fight the desire to ask questions. I just need to surrender and let the day take its course.

"Hey. I can't even spell or pronounce where we're going today," I say, trying to lighten up a bit with a change of subject. "How you say, ''Gyeongbokgung' Palace? Guy-On-Back-a-Goon? Am I close? Sounds like I'm speaking in tongues."

Mei tries to smile and shakes her head, emitting her typical sigh. "What will I do with you? You no need pronounce, just take photo and have fun!"

Then, on a more serious note, I bring it back. "You know what, Mei? I've been where you are." I place my hand on hers. "I understand more than you know." And with that confirmation, the subject of abuse, fondling or childhood pain is not brought up again. My way of processing these days is not to fix, intervene, or therapize, but to totally surrender my heart, mind, and soul to a bigger Holy Spirit intervention.

Walking out to the bus from the terminal, we pass a huge mirror, and I take a quick glance at my haggard appearance. I laugh out loud. Mei looks perfect, of course, showing no signs that she's been on a fourteen-hour flight. I look like a cross between Pig Pen and Kramer.

"You look fine, Missasue." Mei nudges my shoulder. "Why you worry?"

"Because I want my pictures to look good. I have an audience at home to impress." I smooth my hair—or at least try!—and await her incoming response. Mei doesn't disappoint.

"You have audience? What kind of audience? You mean someone actually want to see and follow you? Go figure!" Then she bellows out this ridiculous sounding giggle.

"You hurt me, Mei. I am devastated. I'm gonna delete you from my Facebook."

"That okay. I no even have Facebook. Waste of time. Too much homework."

Mirrors, texting, social media, and iPhones make for a perilous convergence for me. My husband Jeff was trying to take a photo of his new flat screen television in our bedroom. There's a sentimental attachment to this TV, and he wanted to send the photo to his sister, Susan. I had just stepped out of the shower and could see he was having difficulty getting a focused shot. I, being the tech expert, snatched his phone from his hand, stood back, and took a more panoramic shot of the TV. I handed it back to him and said, "There you go." Problem solved! Photo sent.

After the *swoosh* of the "send" sound, I heard my husband say, "Uh-oh". He was looking at the panoramic picture I had just taken of his TV, his face a mix of cringe and panic.

In the right side of the photo was a reflection: a reflection of me, in the mirror beside the TV. Yes, me, in all my naked glory! *Panoramic* is an understatement. Jeff quickly followed up with a text to Susan that said, "Whatever you do, don't look at the photo I just sent". However, any member of the Homo sapiens species with a brain stem would naturally look after such a command.

Well, I just about died. Fortunately, when Susan saw it she immediately deleted it from her phone. Nevertheless, knowing my family and how our lives are so Facebooky, I shiver at the thought of how easily my "awesomeness" could have appeared online! Ugh. Dear God help us all.

The best part of the story was Susan's Facebook post the next day—and I quote:

"My advice for today...Always take the time to check your 'reflection' before sharing with the world! You never know what you may find...Only so many will TRULY ever understand...LOL!"

I chimed in:

"I've always desired to 'reflect' the love of Christ in all I do...just saying!"

Then my friend Tami, who I enlightened to the course of events, added:

It is so valuable to bare our souls, even our very beings in a total act of vulnerability. Yay, verily I say even beyond transparency to allow others to behold our unveiled state. Can I get a witness??

Hilarious. And it didn't end there. I commented:

Reading from today's devotion – '...see the Light of My Presence shining on all your circumstances....'

Yes, the light was shining on two very large circumstances, I might add.

I surrender all

Surrendering means to give in or give up, and even, in some cases, give away. Years ago, our family went out for dinner at a popular restaurant in the Dutch country of Pennsylvania. One of the exceptional specialties on the menu was chicken potpie. We could not wait to taste the tender chunks of dough in a savory gravy with melt-in-your-mouth chicken tenderloins. Simply scrumptious and, of course, very fattening.

As the server-in-training nervously approached our table, she smiled and glanced at my mother first. My mother announced, "I'll have the chicken potpie". Within a second, my father joined in, "You know, I'll have the chicken potpie, too".

The young waitress looked past me and went straight to my husband who was holding up three fingers, proudly, and saying, "No question here— I'll do the same. Make that three, and I'll also have a large Coke."

The server's responsive giggle should have given us some clue or warning of what was to come, but we didn't pay any attention. She said, "Wow, you're gonna need that large Coke."

Moments later our order arrived, and we noticed our waitress relying on the aid of another waitress to haul the two trays filled with plates. One plate of chicken potpie for my dad, one for my mother, and three orders of chicken pot pie for my husband!

At first, we were stunned, then we all started laughing, realizing the server didn't understand that "make that three" meant Dad wanted one, my mom wanted one, and my husband's order made three total!

We still don't think she fully understood. Trust me, it has been a longtime family joke. I'm just glad I didn't say, "Hey—make that four!" We would have had nine plates of chicken potpie on our table.

Here's what I know, and I'm sad to report: Many Christians leave their generous and pleasant attitudes in the car when they dine out. The owner of a popular restaurant in town told me that her staff shudders with fear and discouragement when they know a Christian conference is in town. One of the managers said, "Some of these Christians are the worst. They don't tip well, and they always complain. It feels like we can never do anything right for them."

By all means, we probably have had good reason to complain about the wait staff at some eating establishments, but that doesn't give us permission to be mean, cruel, or stingy. Here are a few things to think about:

1. Most servers get a meager salary, and they depend solely upon their tips for survival. Keep that in mind when deciding what percentage to tip on your bill. We usually go with 20%, 20% + $1 for exceptional service, and only 15% when service is substandard or barely adequate. Most smart phones come with a calculator, and there are apps that help figure out tipping.

2. If your food doesn't appear to be exactly what you ordered, or is not good, remember most mistakes can be easily corrected, and whatever is on the plate happened in the kitchen (the server is not responsible). I've seen many people not leave a tip for the server when something went wrong in the

kitchen, when in fact the manager should have been alerted to the trouble.

3. In support of a server-in-training, smiling or saying "good job" goes a long way.

One server told me she would never go to a certain church in town, because when congregants convened at the restaurant after church services, they were rude, harsh, cheap, and not very compassionate. This has got to stop!

As I travel the roads and eat in hundreds of restaurants a year, I am on a mission to dispel the bad rap that many Christian consumers are earning. Share a smile, show generosity, yield, surrender to being more friendly—and take the time to learn and *say* the name of your server. You'll be amazed at the service you receive.

What does all this restaurant talk have to do with surrender? In my mind, it's all about surrendering our right to be served, to be satisfied consumers, to be superior. What would Jesus do in a restaurant? Just as He did throughout his life and ministry, I think He would surrender his right to be God, his right to be served. Who are we to offer anything less?

As I walked out of one restaurant on a recent East Coast trip after leaving a particularly generous tip, the server ran out to the parking lot to thank me. She told me she was on a break and said, "Thanks for the tip and for making me laugh".

When I told her I felt like God wanted me to give her the money, she started to cry, right there, the two of us standing beside my car. "Are you okay?" I asked her.

"No," she said, "I need prayer. Do you have time to pray with me before you leave?"

I took the time. And she actually surrendered her heart to Jesus in that prayer. That is a restaurant story I will never forget.

Luke 6:37 (MSG), says:

Don't pick on people, jump on their failures, criticize their faults—unless, of course, you want the same treatment. Don't condemn those who are down; that hardness can boomerang. Be easy on people; you'll find life a lot easier. Give away your life; you'll find life given back, but not merely given back—given back with bonus and blessing Giving, not getting, is the way. Generosity begets generosity.

A Prayer of SUErrender

"God, help me never to take for granted this generous life you've given. Help me center my heart by surrendering to you daily. You are my hiding place. You will preserve me from trouble. And You will surround me with songs of deliverance, at just the right time. Make me totally aware when I resist or demand rather than surrender.

～

I know I'm being watched by Mei this entire day in Seoul. We see some pretty amazing architecture. We eat at two little restaurants, and I'm afraid to even ask what I ate at that sushi place. But I smile and surrender to the euphoria of the day. I start to leave a tip on the table for the server, and as I take money out of my wallet, Mei grabs the ten-dollar bill and says, "Put that back. That too much." She then goes into her thin satchel and pulls out a bill of some sort, equal to about five dollars, and we're off to our next stop. I flinch inside a little to think of stiffing a server, but in this instance I surrender to the cultural ways of my tour guide.

"The Lantern Festival is happening now," Mei says. "Would you like to see?"

"Oh, that sounds pretty cool." I have no idea what I am about to see.

Imagine the scene: Enormous ornate structures floating in the sky, and 100,000 locals outfitted in traditional Korean dress (Hanbok) performing dances, offering prayer and carrying indescribable illuminated lanterns in shapes of flowers, animals, fruits and other Buddhist symbols. Lanterns of red and yellow lighting up on the ground and in the sky and an occasional "lift off" of a kite-like lantern or two. I am spellbound and enchanted by the scene. All this happens in one of Seoul's busiest streets. What a colorful magical sight.

Mei looks to the sky and says, "If we release them, they must go somewhere. They beautiful, but so fragile. They must be held by the master of the string. But to be released and to be free, they must let go."

Wow. I don't dare move or make a sound at this point. Talk about surrender. I have to relinquish my interjection of thought, because truly, nothing could have been any truer or more sacred at this point. I stand in awe.

Mei grabs my hand and says, "Missasue? What you need let go of?"

I take a deep breath.

"Oh, Mei, there are many things," I say. "But most of all, I need to release my past into the arms of Jesus. I want to be free of thinking I always have to be *on* or perfect, or constantly the performer. I wish my family and friends could see this. It's a stunning sight, all those colorful flying kites. My photos won't do it justice."

"You'll have more than photo to take home with you, Missasue. You go home changed." Mei squeezes my hand, and then she lets go.

"I'd like to go home changed," I say, "I'd also like to go home WITH change! Didn't we just spend seventy dollars on that sushi back there?!"

"We did, Missasue! And you be better for it. You pay whole bill, I leave tip. That a good deal!" Mei lets out her Mei-laugh, and we leave to return to the airport, our stomachs satisfied and spirits surrendered.

CHAPTER NINE

"SUEpernatural"

Getting back to Incheon Airport after a long day of touring Seoul isn't easy. I am elated and relieved that Mei understands the lay of the land and can speak a few languages. For some reason, though, we miss our shuttle bus back to the airport. It's probably my fault for drinking way too much water and needing to find potty stops every twenty feet.

"Missasue, don't blame yourself. We get taxi."

Now, to me, the word "taxi" means a car. The kind with an engine, a trunk, and headlights, you know. That is not Mei's definition of "taxi," for her ride of choice is a man on an overextended, rusted-out, dissected bicycle with a high back, narrow wooden "bench" just wide enough to perch a magpie. A South Korean magpie at that, which, coincidentally, is their national bird.

I stand there looking between this "taxi" and my tour guide. "And we're going to ride this thing to the airport—for three miles?"

"Yes, Missasue. You sit up on the birdie perch, I hold on to back of driver."

I'm really sorry I don't have a picture of this. Please understand, I'm not a hundred pounds anymore. Most of me hangs over everything. And it was the "everything" suspended, flesh and flubs and everything else, hanging over the "birdie perch" that really was quite impressive. We were jostled and jived for over an hour on back roads that can't be compared to anything I've ever experienced in the U.S. The pedal driver weaved in and out of traffic like a NASCAR driver on steroids. I got very spiritual and found Jesus all over again, praying nonstop until we arrived at the terminal. Our driver wasn't out of breath when we arrived, but I sure was winded.

The process of checking in (again) and going through the security checkpoints also has me a little more than worried. We only have an hour and a half before our gate will close and our flight to Kuala Lumpur may leave without us. But having Mei with me calms my fears. She really knows her way around the international travel rigmarole.

"It a little different this time, Missasue," she says. Mei, I've realized, rarely looks me in the eye. She does a rapid eye-blinking thing—her signal that we'd better hustle! "Because we fly into KL tonight, and it a Muslim country, be ready to answer questions. But do not say much."

I already know not to divulge too much unnecessary information, as an American Christian. It's not that I have anything to hide, but the last thing you want to do is volunteer statements, like, "Hi, I'm on a missions trip to Malaysia, and I hope to share Jesus with all the heathens." Not a good thing to say. As I approach the security agent, with my American passport in hand, a flight itinerary, and a few splinters in my rear, she glances at me and says, "You a social worker?"

I pause for a second, thinking, *Well, yes, I am social and I am a worker, so therefore I must be a social worker.* I nod yes. Mei quickly removes herself from my zone and breezes through the checkpoint. She's waiting for me a few feet away, watching my exchange with the security agent with one curious eyebrow raised.

I'm holding my breath, bracing for more questions. The agent takes the perforated part of my ticket and says, "You go to gate D34."

I skip away from security in a hurry to catch up with Mei. She's walking ahead of me at a brisk pace, but her head is turned toward me and she is talking out of the side of her mouth.

"Since when you *social worker*, Missasue? Hmmm?"

"Since about five minutes ago." I let out a nervous giggle.

I had no intention of fudging the truth there, but it got me through the checkpoint fast. I remember in preparation for this trip, Carrie suggesting that I should never say I'm "going on a missions trip" or that I'm a "missionary" or anything of the sort. Especially when I go to and from Malaysia. I actually felt quite proud to be a social worker—for about two minutes, anyway—

and mostly so relieved the security agent didn't ask any open-ended questions to which I would have had to supply an incriminating answer. God had it covered.

The supernatural hand of God is beyond comprehension and defies explanation. Back in the Seventies, during the gas crisis, Jeff and I were on the road quite a bit. The only days you could purchase gasoline were on odd or even days, depending on the last number digit of your license plate number. We were odd. (Of course we were!), which meant we could buy gas on the 1-3-5-7-9 (you get the idea) days of the month.

It was an autumn day, way back when Tony Orlando and Dawn were tying a yellow ribbon 'round the old oak tree on our radio. Jeff and I were driving home from a work trip on Interstate 81 through Virginia, and our tank was very low. Nearly running on fumes, down to only a few gallons left, we had a choice to make: it was either stop along the road and wait until morning; or keep driving, hoping against hope to find an open gas station.

We began praying and asking God for a miracle. The verse that says to "calleth those things which be not as though they were," from Romans 4:17 (KJV), was being shouted big time in that van. We needed gasoline! As soon as we started praying, we noticed off in the distance at the next exit, an area of lights like a scene from "Field of Dreams." We drove toward the light, and I promise you, right before our eyes were two gas pumps on the side of the road that only accepted dollar bills.

Seriously. An automated gasoline pump! Whoever heard of such a thing in the Seventies?! Such a device didn't exist, that we knew of—or did it?

We jumped out of the van and filled up our gas tank using our cash box money, feeding the miraculous machine dollar bill after dollar bill. What makes this story more supernatural: We could never find those gas pumps again. In fact, we never saw that exit off of I-81 again, either. And we have done some serious road warrior driving up and down that I-81 corridor. And believe me, we searched. That divine fuel intervention goes down as one of our most favorite stories of God's provision in our time of need.

My mother, in her final stages of life here on earth, had a miraculous story, too. Even though she was dying of multisystem failure in her body, she never smelled bad. This is a mercy on a couple of levels. You see, my mother had this innate ability to smell things a mile away. I'll never forget how she would sniff our hair as kids to see if we had washed it, or how she would never stay in motels or places that reeked of decay or mold. It was just her way. She was a super-smeller.

It was so like God to honor my mother in her final stages, to smell like a fragrance of lavender or roses or something just as sweet. It was incredible. Many of the nursing staff would comment, but some weren't too impressed. Those of us who knew my mother and her relationship with God knew that something supernatural was going on in her body, even unto death. "A sweet smelling savor; the fragrance of Christ," some would say. I knew it was God's last chance to show off in the life of a woman who knew Him and served Him well.

I enjoyed a wonderful, spontaneous conversation with a friend the other day. We ran into each other outside a grocery store and stood talking in the June sun for an hour or so, right there in the parking lot. We caught up on each other's lives, chatting about our kids, our mission, our age problems, and everything else you can think of. It was as if God appeared out of nowhere, giving us both a big hug.

As we were saying our goodbyes, I realized I had frozen groceries in the car. I said to my friend, "Oh gosh, I've got salmon in the car." Nothing like the smell of fish on a hot day. And in your car, ick!

My friend stared at me a second. "Oh, you better go," she said. "How long is he in town for?" I paused, realizing the great comedic opportunity served up right before me, and said, "Oh, at least till supper."

We're still laughing over that one. I'm not sure who she thought I had waiting in the car, and I'm not insinuating that comedic response is supernatural, but it was a great way to see God connect two friends in a crazy moment!

As a kid, I saw both of my grandmothers pray for everything. And when the hand of God moved in a situation or friends' lives, they were never surprised. In fact, to them, it was normal. When prayer was all you had, especially in the wee hours of the morning with no doctors, I remember my grandmothers praying and interceding for my brother and me. High fevers would diminish; coughing or sick stomachs would ease—just because they prayed and believed God for healing of their grandkids.

Jeff and I have always been moved to give money when it seems we don't have it. The principle of giving has always proved to us the faith we need when the checkbook balance hovers near zero. Time and again, God has blessed us when we have sacrificially given at some of the worst times, financially. I watch how He has taken care of us, when there's no real explanation of how. If nothing more, may you be encouraged today, that God pays attention, big time, when you remember that He—and no one and nothing else—is your source.

I was driving in a massive East Coast snowstorm, coming down from a mountain near Scranton, PA, on my way to Harrisburg. I had just finished a concert and probably should have stayed with the pastor's family, but I chose to get ahead of the storm and onto the next engagement before nighttime. I attempted a shortcut back to the interstate down the mountain, via one of those back roads that hadn't yet been plowed. My little Honda slid all over the road. I had no cell service, either. I didn't panic just yet, but I was starting to feel out of control.

I knew I was only about four miles from the interstate, but those four miles took me almost two hours. I was praying the whole time, shouting to God, "Thank you for making a way! Thank you, God, for making my road passable." In the distance, I could barely make out what appeared to be a small service station. Creeping along at about 3 MPH, I slid into the station parking lot and stopped. I buried my head in the steering wheel and cried. "Thank you, God."

The snow was almost halfway up my door. I pushed it open, muscled my way out, and shuffled to the entrance and into the welcome shelter of the station. When I opened the door, the woman behind the register shouted, "Wow! Where did you come from? The roads have been closed for hours."

"I just came down that hill," I said, pointing behind me, "coming from south of Scranton, on that road up there."

She looked puzzled.

"What road? There's no road coming down from that mountain. Only the interstate."

"No," I said, stomping the snow from my boots, looking around for a hot chocolate maker. "There's a road, alright, and I just came down it."

"I've lived here for twenty years, and I don't know of any road that goes down that mountain where you're pointing to, except on the other side."

I strained to see through the steamed-up window of the station and gestured for her to come over and look. Pointing toward the mountain where I came down, I suddenly realized *there was no road*. No tire tracks either. No proof that I drove down that hill. Unfathomable, incredible, unbelievable—I know. Nothing but snow-covered trees and two feet of snow or more.

She looked at me the way you look at a person who tells you she just saw Sasquatch. "Where you headed now?"

"I'm on my way to Elizabethtown." I fumbled with a styrofoam cup, dispensed hot chocolate into it, and carried it to the counter. "I hear the interstate is plowed and clear heading that direction."

"It is, but you best get going." She looked down at my cocoa. "It's on the house. Just be safe." I smiled and nodded, still dazed. "And don't be makin' no more roads!"

I didn't fully realize in that moment, or for some time, how God "made a road, where there ain't no road." It baffles me even as I write this now, but it's true. There's no other explanation. The supernatural hand of God helped me at just the right time.

Almost a decade ago I wrote a song called "Steppin' Out." Let me tell you, it was never in my plan to write a line dance song. But as soon as I performed it live for a group of women in Boston, the rest was history. They jumped, they danced, and they created their own formation! We were all *literally* stepping out, just like the song says. It was a sacred Electric Slide moment!

The rumors spread. Sue Duffield is dancing in church. Oh, and she's not just dancing at women's events, she's strutting her stuff in Sunday morning corporate worship services in some of the most conservative churches in America. (GASP!) My Baptist friends were like, "What?!"

I chuckle when I see promotional material that says, "Have Sue Duffield come to your church for inspirational line dancing and devotion!" Hilarious. The funny part—I can't even dance.

At a women's event in West Virginia a young woman decided she wanted to line-dance with me on stage. I didn't know her story but as she made her way to the front, I could see that she'd suffered a stroke. What I did not know yet was that this was her first outing in six months since her rehab and therapy. I also was not prepared for how God miraculously healed her in front of us all!

Seriously, she started to move her muscles, and the more she danced, the more she moved her once immovable left side. The place went wild. No explanation but God.

Don't ask me why I was shocked to see this. The audience came unglued. We were all crying, laughing, jumping, and singing. It was a significant supernatural moment — something I could never orchestrate, dream up, or prepare for. The church had been going through some real drama in their women's group. Now, those women were getting out of their seats, weeping, and asking forgiveness of one another.

I stood there in the wake of my own repentance because God was doing some serious shaking in me, too. It was the mending of hardened hearts and broken lives. Only God could take something so controversial, so out-of-the-box, and so fun like line dancing in church (!) to make His presence known.

The lyrics of "Steppin' Out" come from the book of Revelation.

> God's opening doors that no man can lock,
> And He's locking doors no one can open
> He says I see what you've done;
> Now see what I've done
> I've opened the door that no man can shut.

Revelation 3:7-8 (MSG) says "Write this to Philadelphia, to the Angel of the church. The Holy, the True—David's key in his hand, opening doors no one can lock, locking doors no one can open—speaks:

"I see what you've done. Now see what I've done. I've opened a door before you that no one can slam shut. You don't have much strength, I know that; you used what you had to keep my Word. You didn't deny me when times were rough."

It's easy to assume that this specific revelatory word to the church of Philadelphia in Scripture is just for those unspiritual doors, or doors that represent chaos—even doors of protection, maybe. Closed doors often seem to represent protection, like a holistic or preventative "stop". But what if those doors are the unrealized opportunities of the "go" in your life? What if the closing of the one door you have the greatest grip on is really the answer you're looking for?

For years I held on to the handles of "closed doors". They never opened. I tried to budge them, pull them, push them, and even jump up ON them, screaming like a kid hanging on with both hands and feet to break down that door. I still held on to hopes for commercial success or at least some sort of Christian music/publishing industry recognition. Ironically, when I finally let them go, I walked away, realizing those doors weren't for me.

A unique new door began to open for me. And this was the door I will call "Prepared". Like the synchronization of those airline doors shutting, I felt the whooshing sound of new ones opening, as if to say, "You weren't ready before. Now you are."

Am I the keeper of my doors, or is God? The no's and the closures are just as strategic as the yes's and the openings. Gather all the strength you have, open your hands and heart, and let go. I mean really let go. Unfold, unlock, unfurl, and unfasten your will into His. Take a deep breath and anticipate God enfolding you, guiding you, and loving you like crazy.

1 Corinthians 15:42-44 (MSG) says:

This image of planting a dead seed and raising a live plant is a mere sketch at best, but perhaps it will help in approaching the mystery of the resurrection body—but only if you keep in mind that when we're raised, we're raised for good, alive forever! The corpse that's planted is no beauty, but when it's raised, it's glorious. Put in the ground weak, it comes up powerful. The seed sown is natural; the seed grown is **supernatural**—*same seed, same body, but what a difference from when it goes down in physical mortality to when it is raised up in spiritual immortality!*

A SUEpernatural Prayer

"Dear God, help us to always know that none of us lives to himself alone and none of us dies to himself alone. If we live, we live to the Lord; and if we die, we die to the Lord. Whether we live or die, we belong to You. May we gaze with open eyes and an open heart, ready at any time for your supernatural intervention, making a way for us. May we believe that You always are working for our good."

~

Our final flight from Seoul to Kuala Lumpur is a quiet overnight flight of about six hours. Our seat assignments change at the last minute, separating Mei and me. She makes a frowny face from 16C. I send her an air kiss from 22B and mouth, "We'll connect when we land."

I can't wait to see Carrie and Mindy. I am on pins and needles waiting to land in Malaysia. I try to sleep most of the way, but struggle to get comfortable. I pop a few Tylenol PM's, hoping that will help. All it does is make me drowsy, and my bottom lip numb, but not enough to fall asleep. I can see Mei and notice that she is almost completely stationary in her seat. She hardly moves a muscle. She must be asleep, and I begin to wonder if I just plain wore her out. I should be the one all worn out! My body aches from Mei walking me all over Seoul, but my mind can't rest.

I get out my mother's Bible again and begin to leaf through the pages. I flip to the back few pages and see where she has written notes and jotted a few messages from sermons. My eyes fall on something I haven't seen before, in my mother's handwriting: *"You will never lack anything when your hand is in God's hand."*

How did I miss that? I close her book and whisper to myself, "Thank you, Mom, for being such a huge part of this trip. You loved Carrie deeply. And you loved her mission. I'm going, representing you."

A flight attendant I don't recognize starts roaming the aisles, and this time she quietly stops by my seat. "Sorry you not sit by you friend," she says. "We have full plane. You have fun before?"

"Oh, that's okay. I thought I would ask if we could sit together, but it's no problem. She looks like she's fast asleep anyway. And yes, we had a blast in South Korea," I say. "Amazing people."

"Yeah, she dead tired, it looks like, and we landing soon. So where you journey take you now?"

"I'm headed to KL and Petaling Jaya, and maybe to the Philippines. I'm going to see a dear friend who has given her life to helping abused girls and women. I can't wait to see her."

"That very admirable. I hope you change the world. It's different there in Malaysia, that for sure."

We start the descent, and the butterflies are turning in my stomach. I notice Mei stretching her neck around to see where I am. She smiles and throws her hand in the air with a thumbs-up gesture.

There's much debriefing, collecting of luggage, and entrance details to go through. I try, as I deplane, to keep up with Mei. It appears that she has distanced herself from me, or at least that's the way it feels. Maybe this is how she deals with goodbyes. I don't know, but I'm determined to stick close.

I immediately feel the difference. Carrie and Mindy had prepared me for this. There's a vast atmospheric spirituality separation between Seoul and Kuala Lumpur. It feels much darker, much more compression-like. It feels dark, bright, heavy and light; such a vast contradiction, all at the same time.

The first thing I see in the KL airport is a huge sign that says, "Stop Human Trafficking", with a picture of a battered woman and a child. I find that ironic since Malaysia is known to have some of the worst trafficking in the world. A sign like that seems only to appease the world travelers and pacify the tourists. It would be risky to say that aloud, and especially risky to put it in writing. But I do.

Saying goodbye to Mei is going to be tough. I feel it rising up in my throat. It's like she became family to me over the past 24+ hours. Ahead of me she waltzes through customs, because she's Malaysian. I see her waiting for me, and that makes me smile.

As I draw nearer to Mei, I also see Carrie and Mindy waving on the other side of security! I'm ecstatic to see them, while at the same time, sad to say goodbye to Mei. I wave to them and lift my hand to say in a hold gesture, "Just one minute."

I look into those big brown Malaysian eyes, and ask, "How do we say goodbye? Will we ever see each other again?" I'm trying to speak through tears.

"We keep in touch, Missasue." She hands me a piece of notebook paper. "Here's my email, my cell phone number."

I grab the piece of paper like it's a thousand dollar bill. "Yes, we will, Mei. I will pray for you. You pray for me, too?"

"I will. I love you, Missasue." And with that, we hug, and she walks away through the crowd.

I stood still watching her for a moment, hoping she'd turn around to look at me one more time. That's when the terminal started moving. I felt lightheaded. My ears began to hear a silent, low frequency hum; a sound unfamiliar to me. My misted eyes lost focus for a few seconds, but when they refocused, I saw Mei turn around in a slow motion blur, looking right at me this time. As she turned and found me, her face became my mother's face. I stood there blinking and rubbing my eyes, but I promise you this: Mei waved back to me much like my mother used to wave. And her face was definitely Naomi Beatty's face. Only for a second...

I couldn't move. But I knew I had to get to Carrie and Mindy. I *wanted* to get to Carrie and Mindy. I could barely walk to where they were standing, but as soon as I entered their space, we danced and hugged like little girls.

Carrie's first words to me were, "You won't believe this, but my mother is on my cell phone right now, and she wants to talk to you! Hilarious! All the way from Jersey!"

I grabbed the phone. Barb, one of my mother's best friends, said, "So glad you made it safe, honey. You know, your mother would be so proud."

I take an enormous deep breath, brush back my sweet and sad tears, and do a second encore of the happy dance with Carrie and Mindy. I made it. I really made it.

AFTERWORD

"Miss-SUEllaneous"

I have many unanswered questions about those last few minutes at Kuala Lumpur Airport. Did I have a major mesmerizing dream sequence from Atlanta to KL? Did Mei really exist? Was Mei my angel in disguise? Was Mei my mother?

I don't know any of the answers to those questions, but I do believe that the supernatural hand of God was with me—and always *is* with me, and you(!)—no matter what. I know I saw my mother's countenance in Mei's face, if only for a second. It was real, and it was there. She vanished like the wind, too. So much so that four years later I'm still trying to find Mei. Her email returns as "undisclosed" or "incorrect", and her phone number has never worked from the beginning. I even went to great strides to contact the pharmaceutical school in Ohio where she was a student, hoping to find her. Nothing. In fact, the woman on the phone said they'd never had a student registered by that name.

Years ago, I may have pushed my way out of my mother like a cataclysmic eruption—to be separate, set apart, different, and my own person. However, the older I become, the more I feel the tug that she's closer than ever before. I am all over the place, traveling everywhere. I am ubiquitous, it would seem. But I can't wait till one day when I can take that final destination trip and ask God the question, "Was Mei my mother on that flight? Was it a supernatural phenomenon that can't be explained?"

I'll never know until I see God. In the meantime, I make it my life's mission to grasp the unexplainable without question, to expect the supernatural and to run from the conventional.

You, my friend, can rejoice in your own diversity, too. Be exceptional and different. Quit marching to the beat of the so-called acceptable drum. Celebrate the extreme uniqueness that is totally you. You may create quite a stir and storm. You may also have to follow up with a recovery team after you've cleared out their sacred cow path! Remember, it's hard work to be YOUnique. When your own tsunami builds, be prepared to offer yourself solace, comfort, and explanation. Some of the best communicators and storytellers are those who have survived many storms, yet continue to live out life in their own truth and actuality.

Is it possible to laugh and cry at the same time? Of course it is! I'm doing it right now as you read this! I laugh with the healing possibility that your bone marrow will be strengthened and those brittle bones will be dry no more. Why? Because that life giving "laughter does good like medicine" thing is right on. And the tears that flow down my cheeks right now are also proof that my heart aches for you to see Jesus like you've never seen Him before.

Take the plunge, expect the unexpected and brace yourself for an earthly journey that is merely a warm-up act for eternity.

I amuse myself at the term "saint" in the subtitle of this book. As famed guitarist Chet Atkins once said, "I'm only a part-time saint!" That's true for me, too! Together, let's be a full-time uninhibited, unrestrained and abandoned voice of imperfection for the all-perfect Jesus.

Me and Mei Chen
in Seoul, Korea

When Mei turned
back to look at me
in the airport, this is
the face I saw ... my
beautiful mama.

THANK YOU

To my Harley-riding piano-playing husband, Jeff, and my incredibly beautiful adult children, David and Annie - I love you for living, breathing and tolerating all these stories along with me. You've put up with a lot! To my brother, Dave, and my sister-in-love, Susan, and extended family who have labored through this writing process along side me - thanks for pretending you enjoyed it all!

I want to especially thank Jennifer Deshler who encouraged me over two years ago to "write it down." Your expertise and publishing knowledge astounds me. What a true friend you have become. Thanks to Beth Bates who I lovingly call "Beth Bares", who allowed this baring-of-my-soul-journey to take a more precision-like walk through your editing. And a big shout out to Micah Kandros, graphic visionary and design superman. Oh, how we laughed ourselves silly on that infamous photo shoot day!

I have been blessed and influenced by great communicators and connectors like Dave Kyllonen, Neil Enloe, Duane Nicholson, Phil Enloe, Dave Bailey Sr., Dan Betzer, John and Esther Hamercheck, Jonathan Willey and Alan Bosmeny. What an impact you've had. And a special thanks to Tim Enloe who got me thinking I need to write a book.

Last of all, and surely not least, I am blessed with an incredible circle of awesome women, who, as iron sharpening iron, mold me, invest in me and love me in spite of myself! Thank you, Dawn Vagle, Donna Bosmeny, Tami Heim, Linette Willey, Candy Davison, Stephanie King, Carla Pitman, Nora Clark, Lois Panner, Cookie Kaluka, Elvira Kern-Waynick, Janet Fabian, Chris Bonno, Cheryl Spicer, Toni Birdsong, Sandra Heska King, Linda Bennett, Marie Armenia, Wendi Miller, Suzie Pope, Amy Stevenson, Lynn Montgomery, Jackie Benicky, Jennifer Wilkerson, Tami Stevens, Barbara Ayars, Donna Hough, Candy Christmas, Carrie Baber, Mindy Baker, Donna Halliday, Gini Moritz, Linda Hobbs, Odessa Hawley, Karyn Harshbarger, Ruth Enloe, Judy Kyllonen, Jean Ann Nicholson, Katy Moore, Mary Jo McElravy, Jan Enloe, Betty Holmes, Nancy Pfister, Fran Sandidge, Susan Sitzes, Donna McNee, Terri McCoy, Barb Baber, Donna Reed, Gail Giordano, Susan Jensen, Kaye Wireback and all the women's ministries of these incredible churches - First Assembly of God, Penns Grove, NJ, Five Rivers Church of Elkton, MD and Resting Place Church of Nashville, TN.

Interested in having Sue come to your event, church, women's retreat or conference? Send an email to: radiosue@me.com

Connect with Sue online:

Twitter: @sueduffield
Facebook: facebook.com/sueduffieldministries
Instagram: @sueleeduffield